CARDIFF
A Maritime History

CARDIFF
A Maritime History

JOHN RICHARDS

TEMPUS

First published 2005

Tempus Publishing Limited
The Mill, Brimscombe Port,
Stroud, Gloucestershire, GL5 2QG
www.tempus-publishing.com

British Library Cataloguing in Publication Data.
A catalogue record for this book is available from the British Library.

ISBN 0 7524 3568 X

Typesetting and origination by Tempus Publishing Limited
Printed in Great Britain

CONTENTS

LIST OF ILLUSTRATIONS

PREFACE AND ACKNOWLEDGEMENTS

The Marquess of Bute's Docks were the heart of Cardiff and central to the development not only of the city but also of its hinterland. The port became of worldwide importance and Cardiff ships and men made their way to any place where a cargo might be found.

This book aims to provide an account of Cardiff's maritime past – the earliest stirrings of seaborne trade, the cargoes of wool, hides and butter and the ubiquity of piracy. Rapid growth came through the town's role as a port exporting iron from the works around Merthyr Tydfil, and a booming trade in coal led to further expansion, with the building of new docks at Cardiff and Penarth. There were tragic losses in the two world wars, which were to be followed by a sharp decline in the demand for south Wales coal. Linked with changes in the nature of the port's trade were developments in the vessels carrying the cargoes – from sail to steam to motor, and the introduction of faster and larger ships.

Size of vessels

It is helpful to have some indication of a vessel's size. In this text this is done in two ways: the length and breadth in metres may be given and, more often, the tonnage is noted after the name – for example *Peterston* (2,768). The problem is that the way tonnage was calculated changed over the centuries, so that tonnage figures for different periods may not be strictly comparable. In medieval times ships came to be described by the number of tuns they could carry, a tun being a cask which could hold over 200 gallons of wine. Later, a formula based on the vessel's length, breadth and depth of hold was used to work out the 'tuns burden'. From the middle of the nineteenth century a new measurement system became standard.

In this book the figure given for a vessel is, where possible, that of *Gross Registered Tons*: the volume of all the enclosed spaces (such as bunkers, holds and deck-houses) of the vessel calculated in cubic feet, and 100 cubic feet are assumed to equal 1 ton.

There are other ways of measuring tonnage: *Net Registered Tonnage*, for example, is a vessel's 'earning space' – that which is available for cargo and passengers. It is the Gross Registered Tonnage minus the space taken up by, for example, bunkers, crew accommodation and engines.

Acknowledgements

The writer of a work such as this inevitably relies upon many earlier publications and those found to be of particular relevance have been listed in the bibliography. The author is grateful for the help given by members of the staff of: The British Library; Bristol Industrial Museum; Cardiff Library Service; Centro de Documentation Maritima, Museo Maritima Barcelona; Dundee Central Library; Glamorgan Record Office; Glasgow University Archive Services; Langsdale Library, University of Baltimore; Lewisham Local Studies Library; Library of Congress; Liddle Collection, Brotherton Library, University of Leeds; Mission to Seafarers; Museum of Welsh Life; National Museums Liverpool; National Library of Wales; United States Naval Historical Centre; Vale of Glamorgan Libraries.

Thanks are due to the following for permission to use illustrations from their collections Associated British Ports 73, 74, 75. Bristol Industrial Museum 29, 51, 53, 59, 60, 64 Dundee City Council, Central Library, Photographic Collection 43. Glamorgan Record Office 11, 18, 24. Glamorgan Record Office and South Wales Record Society 4. Glasgow University Archives Service 28. Campbell McCutcheon 46, 47, 54, 55. National Library of Wales 27. National Museums Liverpool 44. Newport City Council Museums & Heritage Services 1. Njcpublications.demon.co.uk 61. Rhondda-Cynon-Taf Libraries Photographic Archive 5, 7. Society of Antiquaries of London 3.

1

THE SEVERN SEA

The first people to venture upon the Severn Sea did so in boats made from hollowed-out tree trunks, or of hide stretched over a wooden frame, or from planks sewn together with thread and caulked with moss. An oak plank from this kind of boat – dated to about 1700 BC – was found at Caldicot, about twenty miles from Cardiff, and the remains of a smaller vessel from around 1000 BC turned up at nearby Goldcliff. Both were propelled and steered by paddles, and were similar to other excavated Bronze Age craft, such as those at Ferriby on the Humber. Boats like these were still in use when the Romans arrived at what is now Cardiff and erected a fort, in around AD 55–60, near the river. Easy access by water must have been an important consideration for those deciding where to site this new military base, and the sea was a key factor in Roman plans for controlling the region. Signal stations were set up on the West Country coast, and ports developed at Crandon Bridge on the River Parrett and at Abona (the present-day Sea Mills) on the Avon. The principal port for the region was probably at Gloucester, with harbours on the Welsh coast at Caerleon, Cardiff, Neath and Carmarthen. There were, of course, any number of natural landing-places, such as beaches and estuaries, many of which would remain in use by small vessels right up to the twentieth century, but Roman Cardiff would have needed a well-built quay to cope with boatloads of building materials and the heavy traffic of soldiers, animals, traders and goods. From about 300 AD a fleet was stationed on the Severn to counter a growing piracy threat, and Cardiff may well have been a base for the vessels, which would have needed good harbour and shore facilities.

A find in November 1993 at Barland's Farm, near Magor, throws light on the sort of boat in use by local Romano-British people in the late third century. Constructed of sawn planks fastened together with iron nails, it was caulked with tar mixed with crushed wood. Worked by a crew of three, with a mast and sail, the vessel was probably about 11.40m long, 3.16m wide, with a depth of 0.90m and capable of carrying, say, four dozen sheep, or perhaps a hundred bags of grain.

Maritime links were developing between Wales and Ireland, although during the middle years of the third century communities around the Severn Sea came to fear attacks by Irish raiders. The early Welsh Church had particularly close ties with Ireland, and devotees sailed across St George's Channel to study and to preach. In the sixth century St Illtud founded a religious centre at his birthplace, Llanilltud Fawr (Llantwit Major), which grew into one of the most celebrated in the British Isles. Among the

1 A model of a third-century vessel, reconstructed on the basis of finds from Barland's Farm, near Newport.

scholars was St Samson of Dol, a Welshman who travelled to Brittany, founded a monastery, and became a bishop. Another alumnus was Gildas (*c*.495–*c*.570) who, in *De Excidio Britanniae*, describes the Severn as one of the routes by which 'of old, foreign luxuries were wont to be carried by ships.' Contemporary with Gildas and Illtud was the high-status family living at Dinas Powys, which enjoyed the use of olive oil, wine and pottery imported from France and the Mediterranean. Excavations at the nearby monastery of Llandough found the remnants of amphorae, used for storing olive oil, which had been made in the Mediterranean area.

In later centuries Scandinavian seafarers followed the same path as the Irish – raiding, then trading, followed in some places by permanent settlement. The *Anglo-Saxon Chronicle* records that in the year 914 a ship-army appeared in the Bristol Channel and raided in Wales 'where it suited them'. Getting into difficulties, the army took refuge on Flat Holm, where many died of hunger before the survivors eventually managed to make their way to Ireland. Depredations went on throughout the tenth century and in 992 Maredudd ab Owain of Deheubarth hired Norsemen to help him mount raids into the territory of Morgannwg, and five years later a Viking army again terrorised Cornwall, Devon and Wales. Traders from Bristol sold slaves to the Scandinavian settlements in Ireland, and there is some place-name evidence for a Viking presence in south-east Wales: Cardiff's Womanby Street might be derived from *Hundamanby*, 'settlement of the dog-keepers' and close at hand are the Scandinavian *Lamby*, *Homri*, *Tusker*, *Sker*, and *Flat Holm* and *Steep Holm*.

The Normans

The Norman method of acquiring land was to arrive in force, set up well-defended strongpoints, and then take whatever they wanted. Robert fitz Hamo, the lord of Creuilly in Normandy, become one of the biggest landowners in England in about 1089 when King William Rufus gave him huge estates in Gloucestershire. Four years later, encouraged by the monarch, he mounted an invasion of the lands across the Severn. Use of the sea was important to these latest conquerors, as castles had not only to be built – at Cardiff based on the remains of the old Roman fort – but provided with secure lines of communication. The important early fortresses in Glamorgan were those on estuaries (at Rumney, Cardiff, Ogmore, Kenfig and Neath) which meant, for example, that, when the garrison at Kenfig was under threat, 'palisades' to reinforce its defences could be cut in the woods around Chepstow and brought to the castle by sea. There is a record of 200 picks being sent from Bristol, and in 1185 twenty-four ships carried timber for repairs to the fortifications.

To military domination the Normans added the religious, appropriating Welsh churches and their property, and handing their management and revenues over to religious foundations in England. Llancarfan was given to the abbey of St Peter at Gloucester, while Tewkesbury Abbey (which was itself a new foundation, dating from 1102) took over the church of St Illtud at Llantwit Major, St Mary's in Cardiff, and a good deal of land besides. New religious houses were set up, including those at Neath 1130, Tintern 1131 and Margam 1147. The church at Llandaff was made a diocesan headquarters and rebuilt as a cathedral, with stone being shipped from Purbeck in Dorset, Doulting and Dundry in Somerset, and Box in Wiltshire.

As well as the carriage of goods, there was by now more frequent sea-borne travel by passengers between south Wales and the west of England, and the new monasteries had 'mother-houses' in France, which meant that there were more journeys to and from the continent. According to Giraldus Cambrensis (c.1146–1223), pilgrimages to Rome began to be fashionable. Ties with Ireland were becoming even stronger and in the early 1200s the abbeys of Tintern and Whitland set up branches in Ireland.

A settlement grew up around the Norman castle at Cardiff, receiving a charter in the second quarter of the twelfth century from Earl Robert of Gloucester. The point of this grant was to try to encourage trade, and thus increase the Earl's income from rents and market tolls. The burgesses would also benefit because they had 'burgage tenements' – land held in return for rent instead of having to perform tasks for the lord – and enjoyed various other privileges. By the middle of the twelfth century the borough of Cardiff had become the largest in Wales, with a population of about 2,000. The charter allowed the burgesses to trade toll-free in Gloucester and its shire (except for having to pay the king's dues on wool and hides) so vessels traded from Cardiff not only to Gloucester, but also to such places as Newnham, Berkeley and Tewkesbury. Further south, Cardiff vessels frequented Somerset harbours such as Watchet, a port from the ninth century, and Dunster, whose harbour is first mentioned in the 1180s. From Bridgwater freight could be carried up the Somerset rivers.

One port, Bristol, was to dominate the economy and maritime trade of the Severn Sea for centuries. In the first half of the twelfth century William of Malmesbury wrote of Bristol as 'the resort of ships coming from Ireland, Norway and other countries overseas', and the trade with Ireland came to be looked upon as the 'prop of Bristol's prosperity'. By the middle of the century quays had been built at Dundas Wharf and shipbuilding was well established. Bristol was so important to the economy of the south Wales monasteries that several of them had premises in the town, encouraged by being exempted from tolls. In 1153 Margam Abbey owned a building within the precincts of Bristol Castle and, over the years, acquired other property and market stalls. The monks of Tintern Abbey are recorded, in 1242, as owning a number of houses and shops.

As a port, Bristol's advantages included being sheltered from the prevailing winds by the Avon gorge and providing a safe anchorage seven miles from the sea, but problems were caused by the great tidal range of the Severn, the winding narrow approach up the Avon, and the silting of the river. The port continued to thrive during the thirteenth century but the facilities were outgrown as trade developed, and it was decided to make a new harbour by diverting the River Frome across St Augustine's Marsh, a project which took seven years. In the new harbour vessels could 'take the ground' – rest on the mud at low tide – and a new stone quay was built with, behind it, 'The Back' (later to become known as the Welsh Back, because so many boats from Wales loaded and unloaded there).

Cardiff at this time had only a wooden wharf and was a minor harbour, with much of what trade there was passing through the various coastal landing-places of Glamorgan and Monmouthshire. References to boats based at Cardiff do sometimes appear in the records, as in 1216 when a Cardiff vessel carrying 'wine and chattels' from Dublin and Drogheda was seized by English officials at Pembroke, and was given by King John to the Earl of Pembroke. The merchants had their goods returned, eventually, but had to pay all the costs of retrieving them. Vessels are mentioned again in 1233, during the rebellion of the Earl of Pembroke against Henry III: 'Several ships of Cardiff and Newport in Wales, and of Bristol in England, were equipped in the manner of galleys, to respectively attack each other; and ships of Bristol and Avereford were then captured'.

Some Cardiff merchants, in 1273, obtained licences to export wool, which was probably from sheep reared on the extensive estates of Margam Abbey. Cardiff was an important place for the White Monks and their lay brothers – both Margam and Neath owned a great deal of property in the town, and land round about. Produce of these estates could easily be exported across the Cardiff quay. In 1250 Margam sold forty-two sacks of wool to merchants of Ghent, and in 1252 sent a cargo of wool to London. Twenty-four sacks of wool were bought in 1271 by a merchant from Douai. (Wool sacks were large – it took four men to lift one).

As well as possessing considerable property, great privileges, and vast agricultural estates, the abbeys were ship-owners. In 1188 Margam Abbey sent a ship to Bristol to bring back corn for 'a very large crowd of beggars' in time of famine. In the 1230s the Neath Abbey's *Hulc* was being sent on trading voyages to England, and Margam's vessels were to be seen in the harbours of Devonshire and Somerset, and were regular visitors to Bristol carrying hides, wool, sheep, cattle and horses, as well as passengers.

The remains of a vessel of this period were found near Magor, fifteen miles from Cardiff, in 1994. Constructed in the middle of the thirteenth century it was clinker-built, with the planks fastened by clench-nails, and was about 14m long and 3.7m in the beam. There was one square-rigged sail, which could drive the vessel at perhaps 6 or 7 knots in a reasonable breeze. Its cargo of iron ore came from the Llanharry area and could well have been brought by pack-horse to Cardiff, to be loaded at the quay.

The Later Middle Ages

By the fourteenth century Cardiff was protected by a stone wall. To the south, between the Taff/Ely estuary and the River Rhymney, were the wet moors and salt marshes which were to be drained during the later Middle Ages. An impetus to the prosperity of the town was provided by Edward II's generosity to Hugh Despenser. The Despensers had their lands in Gloucestershire but saw the lordship of Glamorgan as a good source of further income, making it in their interest to stimulate trade and so increase tax revenues. Most Cardiff trade was still local, but any trade – by land or sea – produced income for landlords. It was recorded in 1296 that Gilbert de Clare had 'toll of markets, as well by sea as by land' and in 1314 there is a mention of 'the toll of timber sold at the port of Cardiff' and worth 33s 4d a year. Anyone using the quay had to pay a fee. In 1324 King Edward decreed that Despenser and the burgesses of his boroughs of Cowbridge, Kenfig, Neath and Cardiff were to be exempt from all taxes on commerce. This was to apply throughout the whole realm, including Aquitaine and Ireland, although the burgesses still had to pay the king's imposts on wool, hides and wine.

From June 1326 Cardiff was a staple port (along with Carmarthen and Shrewsbury) for the export of wool and hides. This meant that all such goods had to pass through the port to make sure that duties had been paid, more ships would have to visit, and the prosperity of the town should increase. This happy state of affairs did not last, as the privilege was removed by Parliament in December 1332. Carmarthen continued as a staple port, and in the 1350s exported about 525 stones of fleeces a year, most of which had to be sent to Bristol or Southampton for transfer to bigger ships to go to Flanders and France.

On 19 April 1340 Cardiff received a charter from Hugh, Lord Despenser, which proved to be important for the growth of town and port. It gave the burgesses some legal advantages, and forbade trading outside markets and fairs. The charter confirmed that two fairs could be held: the Midsummer Fair lasted for a fortnight from 23 June and the Feast of St Mary was held over three days from 7 September. Fairs were designed to promote trade and meant, for the landlords, income from rent for market stalls and tolls paid on transactions. For the customers, the Cardiff fairs provided goods and services not normally available locally as well as excitement, news, gossip, and opportunities for meeting people.

Traders travelled to the fairs by land and sea; they guaranteed a large number of likely customers and the owners of vessels plying from Bristol and Bridgwater (bringing peddlers of 'bridgwaters', a famous broadcloth) would have benefited from the increased traffic. It has to be said, however, that Cardiffians were not always welcoming: in the 1370s John and Lawrence ap Rees and others hijacked two ships near Flat Holm, the *Cristofere* (from Flanders) and the *Nicholas* (from La Coruña) which were carrying wool, general cargo and, according to the Rees brothers, men who were the king's enemies.

For most of the fifteenth century trade was depressed, not helped by the Glyn Dŵr rebellion, the Wars of the Roses, and the loss of Gascony. On 16 September 1400, at Glyndyfrdwy, Owain Glyn Dŵr was proclaimed Prince of Wales, and by 1403 the Welsh had revolted in Glamorgan, laying siege to Cardiff castle and town. But the defenders could still be sustained by sea and the mayor of Bristol despatched a relief vessel with ale, oats, wheat, wine and a thousand 'fishes called hakes... for the men-at-arms and archers there'. Over 500 men were ferried across from Uphill in Somerset and the crown's forces gradually gained the upper hand, with the aid of two vessels commandeered from Neath Abbey.

Travel on fifteenth-century roads was difficult and, when possible, goods were carried by water. Locally, the consignments passed through the main Bristol Channel ports of Bridgwater, Chepstow, Gloucester and Bristol, which was by now second only to London as a seaport. At the top of Bristol's list of imports was wine. William of Worcester in 1480 noted in Bristol Harbour vessels from Spain, Portugal, Bordeaux, Bayonne and Aquitaine, as well as Brittany, Iceland, Ireland, and Wales. William listed the various types of vessel arriving in Bristol from Wales: ships, boats, skiffs, and 'woodbushes, ketches, and picards' arriving from a dozen or so harbours, from Milford Haven round to Chepstow, including 'Cardiff haven'. He described how the Welsh seamen 'moor their ships at The Back on the rising tide, to unload and discharge ships of their goods'.

William of Worcester provides us with an indication of the sizes of fifteenth-century ships at Bristol (see the Preface, above, for an explanation of the tonnage figures given after a vessel's name): *Mary Grace* (300 tons), *The Trinity* (360), *George* (200), *Katherine* (180), *Mary Bride* (100), *Christopher* (90), *Mary Sherman* (54). Most of these were regarded as big ships, in which it was now possible to make longer voyages, in more hazardous waters. The three-masted vessel with square sails had been developed and navigation and sailing techniques had improved, so that it was now possible for Bristol Channel sailors to voyage to Iceland, bringing home cargoes of dried fish. The remains of a fifteenth-century ship, discovered at Newport in 2002, indicate that it was about 25m long and 8m wide at the maximum, made of oak with a keel of beech. Found with it were Portuguese coins and pottery, wooden barrel staves, textiles and stone cannon-balls, as well as remnants of the sails and rigging. The ship was clinker-built in around 1465.

The large ships making their way to and from Bristol could easily be observed from the Welsh shore and many of them would have sought some relief from Bristol Channel gales by sheltering at Penarth Head but, as a harbour operating in Bristol's web, Cardiff was home only to small vessels which went regularly to Bristol and the West Country ports, and occasionally to Ireland.

The Tudor Century

On 7 August 1485 Henry Tudor landed in west Wales. Eighteen days later, at Bosworth Field, Richard III fell and the reign of the Tudors began. It turned out to be a period when seafarers pushed themselves and their ships to the limits, with Europeans extending the boundaries of their known world. Columbus reached the West Indies in 1492; Vasco da Gama sailed around the Cape of Good Hope, discovering the route to the Far East (1497–99); in 1519 Ferdinand Magellan left Seville with 240 men – three years later only eighteen of them returned, the first men to have sailed round the world. John Cabot left the Severn Sea in the *Matthew* to become the first European known to have reached North America (1497) since the Norsemen. In 1577–80 Francis Drake and his men were the first from Britain to circumnavigate the globe. All of these seafarers were in search of profit, for themselves and for their backers. Some, such as John Hawkins, were soon to seek it by transatlantic trading in slaves. His voyage of 1562–3, for example, transported 300 people from the Guinea Coast of west Africa to Hispaniola (now the Dominican Republic and Haiti), where they were exchanged for £10,000 worth of ginger, hides, pearls and sugar. On Hawkins's third journey in 1567–9 many of his seamen were captured, among them forty-year-old Michael Morgan (otherwise known as Morgan Tillert) of Cardiff, who was tortured on the rack in Mexico City and forced to confess that he had been converted to 'Lutheranism'. He was sentenced to 200 lashes. If he survived that ordeal, he was to serve for eight years in the Spanish galleys.

At home, the monasteries were dissolved and their property sold, mostly to the gentry. The 'Acts of Union' of 1536 and 1543 gave even more local control to these gentry families, but ultimate power always rested with the monarch, although in some areas this authority was challenged by Marcher Lords. One right claimed by these lords was that of imposing dues on both cargoes landed and cargoes exported, although the collection process was inefficient and erratic, and a good deal of evasion went on. The lords' agents could be heavy-handed and arbitrary, as a case brought to the Court of Star Chamber in 1538 illustrates. It concerned the ship *Valentine*, a vessel sold by Sir Thomas Sperte, at Chepstow, to Richard Abbys of London, who sold it on to Richard Hore, also of London, who took over the ship at Sanlucar de Barrameda, near Seville.

In August 1530 the *Valentine* arrived at Cogan Pill, with a cargo of wine, salt, alum, and tunny. There, ship and cargo were seized by William Herbert because, he said, duty had not been paid on the cargo and, furthermore, there were fugitives wanted in Portugal on board. Richard Hore was hauled off to gaol in Cardiff Castle but, as the Portuguese passengers had now disappeared into the nearby woods, was released in order to bring them in. Some were apprehended, some could not be found and one, Agnes Fernandez, was dead. Two of the Portuguese accused Richard Hore of being implicated in the death, so he was re-arrested. At the inquest, James, a servant of William Herbert, acted as interpreter of the evidence given in Portuguese. Hore was sent back to gaol, charged with manslaughter, while William Herbert and twenty others took a cruise to Chepstow in the *Valentine*, eating, drinking the wine, and firing the cannon. At Chepstow, William Herbert sold the cargo.

2

EARLY MARITIME CARDIFF

In the early 1550s the Lord Treasurer commissioned Thomas Phaer to report on the 'shipping places' of the Welsh coast. Dr Phaer was Member of Parliament for Carmarthen and then for Cardigan, and described himself as 'Solicitor to the king and queen's majesty, attending their honourable council in the Marches of Wales'. His task for the Lord Treasurer was to find out if the crown's revenues were being collected effectively. On trade in general, Phaer wrote that, 'In all this coast of Cardiff and Glamorganshire is great lading of butter and cheese and other provisions – partly unto other shires of Wales, and partly to Devon and Cornwall and other places. And there goeth away much leather and tallow to the ships of Bristol, and thence overseas without search or control, for they receive it upon Severn without licence or cocket.' (A cocket was a document issued to confirm that customs fees had been paid).

His descriptions of Cardiff, Sully, and Barry are given below.(Some words and phrases have been put into modern English. A 'dry haven' is one where vessels rest on the mud at low tide; a 'road' is deeper water where ships may ride at anchor.)

Cardiff: 'A proper town, walled, where there is a dry haven, and beyond this is a road in the Severn, called Penarth: very good for ships at three fathoms low water. It lies opposite Ashwater and Bridgwater in Somerset... all westerly and southerly winds bring (vessels) in. The towns of Cardiff, and Cowbridge nearby, are replenished with corn and all manner of victuals. And of the port and town, with a goodly strong castle at Cardiff, the lord is the Earl of Pembroke, whose officers claim the right to issue cockets and licences. Memorandum: at this town there used to be a searcher of the King's to restrain all things prohibited, which searcher did sometimes issue cockets himself, and sometimes did allow the lord's to give licence. The last searcher was one Cole, whom your Lordship knew.'(A searcher was a customs official. John Cole had been appointed searcher for the port of Cardiff in 1548, but was not in post for long).

Sully: 'A creek for small boats, which also belongs to the Earl of Pembroke. The Severn is twenty miles wide here.'

Barry: 'A good road: three fathoms at low water; and a dry haven to come into with southerly and westerly winds. It lies opposite Minehead and Bridgwater in Somersetshire.' (The lord was the Earl of Pembroke).

Thomas Phaer's report showed that the whole of the Glamorganshire coast was controlled by the Earls of Pembroke and Worcester. There was no royal customs officer and crown revenues were not being collected. The problem was addressed in 1559 by an Act of Parliament which ordered that, in future, goods were to be discharged or loaded only at certain places. Three 'head ports' were designated – Chester, Milford Haven and Cardiff – responsible between them for the whole coast of Wales. The port of Cardiff stretched from Chepstow to Worm's Head on Gower, with chief customs officers being stationed at Cardiff itself, and deputies at 'member ports'; there were also 'creeks', where there were no regular customs inspections.

In June 1559 Henry Morgan was appointed searcher at Cardiff, the first royal customs officer there since John Cole, over a decade earlier. It was an unpopular and dangerous job: in 1561 Henry Morgan boarded the *Saviour* of Minehead, a vessel owned by Maurice Mathew ('gentleman' of Barry) and William Dawden. Morgan alleged that these two, with Jevan Jones, were involved in exporting 150 barrels of butter without a licence. When Morgan went on board, in Barry roads, James Mathew (Maurice's son) drew a knife and threatened to pin Morgan to the mast; Richard Jones then manhandled the searcher, who feared that he was about to end up in the sea. In the end, the forces of law prevailed, the ship was seized, and was left in the custody of Thomas John Dee, constable of the hundred of Barry.

John Leek, customer (customs officer) at Cardiff from 1563, met problems everywhere and made an official complaint against John Tanner and John Robertes, the Bailiffs of Cardiff, for 'acting as collectors of the Queen's customs in the town of Cardiff', and thus usurping his authority. In 1571 Leek was himself sacked after colluding with smugglers, accepting bribes to release impounded vessels, and extorting money from innocent people. He was not the last bent customs officer, and in 1598 John Millom, controller of Cardiff was found guilty by the Star Chamber of 'sundry foul and notorious misdemeanours and offences', fined £200, and condemned to stand in the pillory.

In the 1550s and '60s more traders began to be charged with attempted evasion of duties. For example:

Robert Vesey of Gloucestershire exported from Penarth tanned leather, calfskins and barrels of butter. The owners of the goods were all from Cardiff – Morgan Mathew, John White, Nicholas Hawkins, Thomas White, John Heymote and John Robertes.

The *Mary* of Walberswick in Suffolk was found to be carrying thirty-nine barrels of butter from Penarth. The butter was owned by the 'alien merchants' Lewis de Pace and Henry Gonsalves of London.

The *Michael* of Sully was apprehended. The vessel's owners were John Smythe, John Webbe (senior) and John Webbe (junior). The contraband cargo belonged to Jevan Jones of Cardiff.

John Tanner and John Robertes were charged with illegally importing tuns of salt. These are, presumably, the two Bailiffs of Cardiff mentioned above who were illegally collecting customs dues.

Thomas White was said to have avoided duty on five tuns of Gascon wine worth ten shillings each, and twelve tuns of salt worth 35s each.

The *Ellen* was owned by William Salter and Richard Sweetman of Bristol. Their offence was the export of seventy-two quarters of wheat at 'Ely Ooze' near Cardiff. The cargo's owners were Miles Mathew 'gent' and William Morgan of Tredegar 'gent'.

The Port Books

When the customs ports were designated in 1559 it was ordered that two sets of 'parchment books' were to be kept – one set for listing details of foreign trade, and the other for the coastal trade. The port of Cardiff kept separate books for Chepstow, Neath, Swansea and Cardiff and they are invaluable as indicators of maritime trade at this time. They have to be used with caution because dues were not always collected, the record-keeping may not always have been punctilious, shipments of livestock were ignored, and the documents are concerned only with 'customable' goods. Trade at smaller creeks and landing-places was likely to escape.

During the latter part of the sixteenth century the kind of vessels recorded at Cardiff were:

Angel (10) of Cardiff. Master: John Raff. Merchant: Thomas Aylworth (Bristol). Bristol to Cardiff. 120 bushels of wheat.

Peter (5) of Cardiff. Master: John Blethyn. Merchant: William Tanner (Cardiff). Cardiff to Bristol. 20 dozen calf-skins.

Peter (6) of Tewkesbury. Master: John David. Merchant: Harry Machyn. Cardiff to Gloucester. Iron, cheese, butter.

Hound (80) of Amsterdam. Master: Jacob Glawsom. Portuguese salt, to Cardiff.

Primrose (30) of Barry. Master: Thomas Clement. Merchant: Harry Chester (Bristol). La Rochelle to Cardiff. Salt and honey.

James (34) of Bristol. Master: John Nicholl. Merchant: Benedick Harrey (Bristol). 3 tons of Spanish iron, 110 barrels of pitch.

William (40) of Cardiff made two or three trips to La Rochelle. Master: Richard Hardie. Merchants: John Tanner, William Wells, Robert Adams. Outward cargoes: lead, coal, Bridgwater cottons. Inward cargoes: pitch, salt, rosin.

John (40) of Cardiff. Master: Phillip Nicholl. Merchants: Robert Adams, William Nayler, John Nonny. La Rochelle to Cardiff – salt.

Moisis (50) of Cardiff. Master: Richard Hardie. Voyages to La Rochelle. Merchants: John Tanner, Robert Adams. Outwards: butter, coal. Inwards: salt, pitch, rosin, figs, prunes.

Angel of Bridgwater. Welsh iron.

Maria (25) of 'Saint Martines' in France. Master: Salamanus Vinion, 'alien'. St Martin's wine and some 'corrupt wine'.

Red Lion (300) of Southampton. Master: William Cornelius. Merchant: Peter Semyne. Ancusan (Enkhuizen in the Netherlands) to Cardiff. Salt, tar and starch.

The trade of Cardiff was mostly coastwise, although there were some larger foreign-going vessels making voyages to ports such as Bordeaux or La Rochelle, taking butter, cloth and perhaps lead or iron. They returned with wine, fruit, raisins, pitch and salt. (In the sixteenth century salt was a very important import because it was used to preserve meat, fish and butter. Regular cargoes were brought to the British Isles from France, especially from La Rochelle).

Most of the coastal commerce was with Bristol, Bridgwater and Gloucester, undertaken by small vessels loaded with butter, cheese, poultry, wool, hides and grain. Bristol was still growing: in 1546 about 6,000 people lived there, but in the next twenty-five years its population doubled, increasing the quantities of food needed from the West Country, and from south Wales.

The occasional shipments of iron from Cardiff, were, as a rule, destined for harbours around the Bristol Channel, and sometimes French or Spanish iron was imported. Various kinds of guns (such as falcons, minions and sakers) were cast locally and sent to Bristol and London, although some found their way to Spain – a trade which the authorities tried to stamp out. Edmund Mathew, who owned the Pentyrch iron foundry, was under suspicion in April 1602 when the authorities urged that 'especial care be had to put down Edmund Mathew esquire for casting any ordnance at his furnace near Cardiff in Wales, because from that place very easily may they be carried into Spain'.

For Cardiff during this period we have a description and a map. The description is by Rice Merrick of Cottrell, near Cardiff, and is from his *Morganiae Archaiographia: A Book of the Antiquities of Glamorganshire*, which was compiled in about 1580: 'The river Taff runneth near the town walls in the west part of the town, and washeth the wall, but somewhat too hard, for part of it is easily overturned, and the sea floweth to the walls where, at the west angle, is a fair quay, to which both ships and boats resort'.

John Speed's map of 1610 indicates the location of the quay, on the east bank of the river near where today Quay Street joins Westgate Street. Cardiff quay was seen as vital to the district's commerce and a report of 1552 stressed that 'the great part of the commonwealth of both town and country resteth on the maintenance of the quay'.

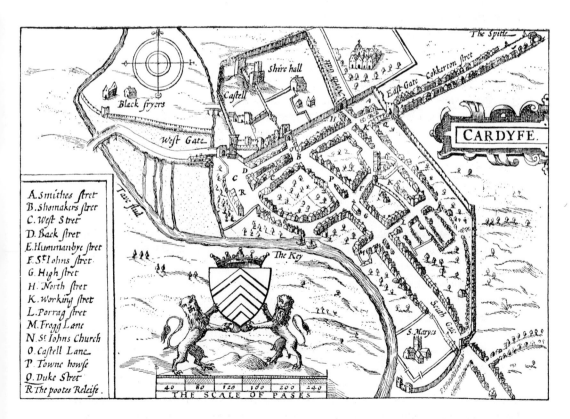

2 John Speed's map of Cardiff in 1610. The quay is on the town side of the river, near the two vessels shown.

CARDIFF: A MARITIME HISTORY

In fact there were now two quays, but the larger vessels had to remain in the deeper water where their cargoes were loaded and unloaded into small boats.

Rice Merrick noted the frequent traffic across the Severn. There was 'continual recourse from Cardiff by sea to Bristol and other good towns in England,' and he lists the other 'ports, havens and creeks of Glamorgan' as being Rumney, Ely, Sully, Barry, Aberthaw, Ogmore, Newton, Neath, Tawe, Oystermouth, Port Eynon and Lougher.

How big were the vessels to be seen at Cardiff? Henry VIII's famous warship the *Mary Rose,* sunk in battle in 1545, was of 700 tons burden, 41m long and 11.66m broad. John Hawkins's fleet on his slaving expedition of 1567–69 consisted of the *Jesus of Lubeck* (700), *Minion* (300), *William and John* (150), *Swallow* (100), *Judith* (50), *Angel* (33), and a pinnace which was towed astern. When Drake set sail for the Caribbean in the 1570s he sailed in the *Pelican* (later called the *Golden Hind*) of 100 tons, together with *Elizabeth* (80); *Marigold* (30); *Swan* (50) and *Christopher* (15). The evidence of appraisals made for the High Court of Admiralty in the 1580s is that 90 per cent of all vessels were of less than 80 tons. As for the boats belonging to Cardiff, the largest were those which made the longest journeys: *John* (40), *Moisis* (50) and *William* (40) made regular voyages to La Rochelle. The Cardiff vessels sailing to Bristol, Gloucester or the Somerset ports were craft such as *Andrew* (14), *Angel* (10), *Godspeed* (10), *Griffon* (10), *Lion* (16), *Margaret* (10), *Peter* (5) and *Speedwell* (10).

Piracy

Piracy is robbery at sea – using force or the threat of force to steal the cargo, or the vessel, or both; some pirates took members of the crew as well. As the volume of trade carried by sea increased, so did piratical activity. In 1450 Sir Henry Stradling of St Donats was crossing the Severn by ferry when he was kidnapped, for ransom, by a pirate vessel from Brittany. Eleven years later John Derell of Cardiff had to find enough money to free his father, also taken by Breton pirates, and raised a thousand crowns by selling wool at Calais.

For centuries the possibility of becoming a victim of piracy was added to the already great hazards of a seaman's life, and the Severn Sea was a particularly dangerous place. In 1578 one of the Queen's own ships was robbed, and merchants from Carmarthen complained to the Court of Admiralty in 1592 that 'four barks of the town in their passage from Bristol to Carmarthen laden with silks, velvets, wine, oil, etc... value £10,000' had been attacked and plundered. The authorities wrung their hands impotently: 'Their Lordships are sorry to learn that the mischief has reached such a height that it can only be checked either by laying the islands and the sea-coast waste and void of inhabitants, or by placing a garrison in every port and creek, which is impracticable'.

Piracy was a multi-national enterprise. At around the time that Sir Henry Stradling was abducted on the Severn by Bretons, some Welsh seamen were brought before a court in Portugal, found guilty of piracy, and sent to prison for ten years. Scottish galleys from the Isle of Barra carried out raids around the western coasts of Britain and into the Bristol Channel, boarding the *White Hart* of Bridgwater in 1580 and stealing cargo worth £1,200. Large numbers of pirates operated out of Irish ports, and Roger Myddleton noted in 1611 that, 'Many of these pirates have their wives and children in these parts'. In the following year five Irish pirates were captured by two vessels sent out

22

from Barnstaple, and the miscreants were made to describe their voyage from Kinsale. The last crew members had joined at Oyster Haven, where John Finch was elected captain. Eventually they arrived at Lundy Island 'to take what they could carry away' – this turned out to be a goat. At sea, they robbed a fishing boat from Clovelly, a ship from London and a pinnace from the Isle of Wight. Sailing on to Milford Haven, they came across two more victims before being caught by the Barnstaple men.

A pirate well known in Cardiff was John Challis, or 'Callice'. Born in Tintern, he was brought up in London, becoming a seafarer as a young man. Turning to piracy, by the 1570s he was selling looted goods (taken with his ship, the appropriately named *Cost-me-Nought*) in Devon. Capturing a Portuguese vessel near the Azores in 1573 he sailed it to Penarth, sold the cargo and bought the *Olyphant,* before returning to sea to harass more merchant ships; again (in 1574) he sold the loot in Cardiff. Two years later he was back with a Spanish vessel, selling the stolen goods to many of the locals, including the customs officer, before going on to seize a Scottish ship called the *Red Lion*. In the same year (1576) Challis's whereabouts were reported to Sir John Perrott, Vice-Admiral of Pembrokeshire. John Davies wrote from Haverfordwest: 'In my journey homeward about Carmarthen I heard that he had passed through Carmarthen towards Cardiff, where he and many other pirates (as is commonly reported) are furnished, vittled, aided, received and succoured'. Goods stolen from Haverfordwest are 'openly sold in Cardiff and other places'.

In 1577 Challis ended up in the Tower of London, but was soon set free, being protected by the powerful Herbert clan. (His father-in-law was William Herbert and he was also in league with Edward Herbert, agent of Sir John Perrott.)

Some attempts were made to track down pirates, and those who helped and traded with them. John Croft was despatched in 1576, with the Queen's commission, to try to capture Challis, but was obstructed at every turn by the authorities in Bristol and Cardiff. Another investigator, Fabian Phillips, arrived at Cardiff in March 1577, referring in one of his reports to 'the great disorders that have happened in these parts upon the sea-coasts by resort of pirates'. The inhabitants of Cardiff and Penarth were, on the whole, uncooperative, but Phillips and his fellow commissioners managed to ferret out the names of a large number of pirates 'that have been received and lodged in this town, and from whom spoils had been had'. William Chick, a pirate, 'a great doer and chief champion among them is happily fallen into our hands'. He refuses to provide information so 'order is taken that he and others shall presently be had to the Council, where the manacles will make them speak'. The customs controller of Cardiff accused David Roberts, John Colchester and others of helping pirates but, Fabian Phillips observed, 'they do absent themselves from their dwelling places since our coming to town, and cannot be found'.

His concluding report contained information about John ap John of Cogan, who was reported to be friendly with pirates: 'He kept them company, as well in his own house, as also by resorting to them on ship board, at taverns and tippling houses in Penarth and Cardiff. He is charged with the receipt of 5 tons of salt, 1,000 dry fish and 200 wet fish of the pirates' spoils'. John ap John confessed that he had been given a caliver (a light, short-range, firearm) by Challis and had bought a tun of wine from David Witty, but pleaded that that he had done only what 'generally all men do' in Cardiff.

Fabian Phillips reported that John Robert ap Euann had been associating with pirates, and that John Thomas, a brewer, gave Challis four tuns of beer in exchange for fish and salt. Robert Adams was another who stocked up with piratical fish and salt. William Herbert admitted that he had victualled the *Olyphant* 'about four years past,' saying that John Challis was his kinsman 'whom he hath favoured and lodged and used oft his company'.

The problem with trying to control piracy was that so many influential people benefited from it and the Lord Admiral himself, who was supposed to combat piracy, made a good deal of money from the cases brought before him. Pardons could be bought. Vice-Admirals generally colluded with pirates and Sir John Perrott, for example, encouraged them to offload their contraband in the ports under his jurisdiction, while some Vice-Admirals sold blank pardons and could be bribed to let captured pirates go free. Many of the gentry snapped up stolen goods, and in 1578 Nicholas Herbert, the Sheriff of Glamorgan, was fined for receiving barrels of fish and salt from pirates and Sir Edward Kemeys (Sheriff of Glamorgan in 1575, 1585 and 1595) appeared in court at least four times.

Sir Thomas Button: Piracy and Exploration

In 1613 Sir Thomas Button was appointed 'Admiral of the King's Ships upon the Coast of Ireland'. He was provided with two small vessels, and with these was supposed to clear pirates from a large sea area, including the Bristol Channel.

Thomas was a member of the Button family of Worleton and Cottrell, near St Nicholas, and thus grew up close to the 'shipping-places' of Cardiff, Barry, Sully and Aberthaw. Like many younger sons of the Glamorgan gentry he decided on a sea-going career, which would be boosted by the patronage of his influential Mansel relatives.

He was at the siege of Kinsale in 1601. Philip II had ordered a Spanish force of about 4,000 to Ireland. Landing at Kinsale, they were bottled up in the town by Queen Elizabeth's troops and eventually surrendered to Lord Mountjoy. Thomas Button was in command of the Queen's pinnace *Moon* and for these services 'on the coast of Ireland' was awarded a pension of 6s 8d a day. Thomas Button then set off on privateering voyages, attacking shipping for profit by the authority of the monarch or the Lord Admiral. It is known that in 1602 he commanded the *Wylloby*, which was owned by two other Welshmen – his kinsman Sir Robert Mansel and Sir John Trevor, the Surveyor of the Navy. The ship arrived home from the Caribbean after a year's absence, with two or three captured vessels and cargoes of valuable loot.

Not long after this he was made captain of the naval ship *Answer* (250), which carried twenty-one guns and was, theoretically, manned by a crew of 100. In fact there were only seventy, with the pay of the missing men being pocketed by Thomas Button and his purser. The incomplete crew had somehow to do the work of the missing thirty men, a situation common to other naval vessels. Sir William Monson was sent in 1610 to deal with Thomas Salkeld (a pirate who called himself 'King of Lundy') but when Monson saw his vessel, the *Advantage*, he found her 'so unserviceable in men, victuals, sails, powder and all things else, that it was impossible to fit her to sea'. One pirate, John Harris, described the crew of a naval pinnace as 'being ragged beggars' with only forty shirts among a hundred sailors.

Thomas Button's fame rests not on combatting piracy, but on exploration. The way to the lucrative markets of the Far East was blocked by the power of Portugal and Spain, so efforts were made to discover an alternative route, perhaps around the north of Canada or Russia. Attempts to open a North-West Passage began with Martin Frobisher in 1576, who was to be followed by John Davis, and then Henry Hudson in 1610–11. Hudson died, but half-a-dozen survivors struggled back, arriving at Gravesend in September 1611, where they announced, falsely, that they had found the North-West Passage.

Losing no time, James I granted a charter to the 'Governor and Company of the Merchants of London, Discoverers of the North-West Passage'. The members, including Thomas Button, were given monopoly rights over the Passage, and preparations were put in hand for a new expedition, the command of which was given to Thomas Button, thanks to his patrons Robert Mansel and John Trevor. His two ships, *Resolution* and *Discovery* left the Thames in April 1612 and made their way to the entrance of Hudson's Bay. After skirmishes with the local people, which left men dead on both sides, the crew sailed on, to become the first Europeans to see the Bay's western shore, which Thomas Button named *New Wales*. They could find no way out towards a western ocean, so they gave the place a name, *Hopes Checked*, and continued their exploration of the coastline. Forced to take refuge for the winter, the men had to abandon the *Resolution*, which was no longer serviceable. At last they were able to continue in one ship, but by July 1613 they had become convinced that there was no North-West Passage through Hudson's Bay and set sail for home.

As a reward for his efforts Thomas Button was made 'Admiral of the King's Ships upon the Coast of Ireland'. He reported on his activities in *A true accounte of services donne by his Majesties shippe the Phenix on the Coast of Ireland, Under my command from July 1614 until this instant January 1622*. In August 1614, a French ship taken by pirates was recovered; in September 1614, a pirate ship of 'Captain Wallsingham' was captured in Lough Fyne. Three months later, ten vessels (including the *Phoenix*, commanded by Thomas Button) and 200 soldiers were sent against the MacDonalds of Islay, destroying galleys and capturing Dunivaig castle.

In the following February Captain Norice was taken, together with seventy of his men, his ship, and twenty-two pieces of ordnance; Norice and six men were hanged in Cardiff. During 1616 three pirate ships were captured around the coast of Ireland, and more than thirty men were executed.

The Merchant Venturers of Bristol described Thomas Button as pre-eminent in trying to suppress 'those common enemies of human society the Turkish pirates', even though his ship *Phoenix* had 'incurred imminent danger… for want of men, the coast of Ireland and Channel of Severn being very dangerous in winter time'. These 'Turks' were, in fact, from North Africa – Barbary pirates – and became a constant menace across the North Atlantic and the Mediterranean. They were frequently of European origin and at the port of Salli, for example, Henry Mainwaring commanded forty ships and 2,000 men, divided into two squadrons under Sir John Fearne and Peter Croston. Between 1610 and 1620 twenty-six Bristol ships were 'taken by Turks' and the Glamorgan butter trade suffered considerably. In 1626 five Cardiff ships were 'taken by the Turkish pirates of Sallie, to the utter undoing of many poor merchants here, and the discouragement of others'. In the first four decades of the seventeenth century the Barbary pirates enslaved about 12,000 people from the British Isles, as well as taking about 800 British vessels. In 1625 these raiders carried off eighty men from Looe in Cornwall and in 1631 a Dutchman, Murat Reis, kidnapped over 100 men, women and children from Baltimore in Ireland.

In 1620 Thomas Button had been allowed a respite from chasing pirates around the Irish Sea. Sir Robert Mansel was ordered to go to Algiers to confront the Barbary pirates in one of their home ports. His Vice-Admiral was Sir Richard Hawkins, and Sir Thomas Button (knighted in 1616) was made Rear-Admiral of a fleet of six royal ships, ten private vessels and two pinnaces. They managed to free only forty captives, and the pirates' depredations continued much as before. At home again, Sir Thomas continued to be favoured, being appointed to the King's Council of War in 1624. He was also a member of a Commission to 'Inquire into the State of the Navy'.

Sir Thomas continued to be responsible for anti-piracy operations on the Irish Sea and in the Bristol Channel, but in February 1634 he was charged with fraud and inefficiency, including failure to prevent the outrage at Baltimore. He was not reappointed to his Admiral's office, which he had held for over twenty years, and died a few weeks later. A friend wrote to the Earl of Strafford, 'Sir Thomas died of a burning Fever, quickly, much discontented that he lost his Imployment in the Irish Sea'.

To the disruptions of piracy were to be added the traumas of civil war, the start of which was signalled when the king raised his standard at Nottingham on 22 August 1642. Charles's armies in south Wales and the west of England were under the command of William Seymour, Marquess of Hertford. Retreating from Sherborne with about 400

3 A meeting of James I's Council of War. Sir Thomas Button was made a member in 1624.

men and forty-five horses, he arrived at Minehead on 23 September 1642, requisitioning some 'Welsh coal boats' to transport his force over to Cardiff. Making Cardiff Castle his headquarters, he set about recruiting more men for the king.

Charles came to Cardiff in June 1645, intent on forming another army after his defeat at Naseby, but most local people were unresponsive – they had had enough of the miseries caused by soldiers and a blockade by Parliament's ships. Following the overwhelming Parliamentary victory at St Fagans on 8 May 1648, 240 of the royalist captives were transported to work on the sugar plantations of Barbados. Seven years later these unfortunates were to be followed to the Caribbean by Henry Morgan, who is thought to have had family connections with Llanrumney Hall, Cardiff. In 1655 he joined the expedition – sent by Lord Protector Cromwell – which seized Jamaica from the Spaniards. After the Restoration, Henry's uncle Edward was made Lieutenant-Governor of Jamaica and, benefiting from his uncle's patronage, Henry Morgan decided to make himself rich. He and his men attacked and looted towns throughout the Caribbean and Central America, including Campeche, Santiago (Cuba), and Granada (in what is now Nicaragua).

In 1668 he led an expedition of twelve vessels, carrying 700 men to El Puerte de Principe (Cuba) and on to Portobello. Two years later Henry Morgan went after the richest prize of all – Panama – with a force of thirty ships and 1,800 men. The town was sacked, and Morgan and his men made off with a fortune in gold, silver and jewels. Henry Morgan invested his share of the booty in large estates on Jamaica, becoming Sir Henry Morgan: Vice-Admiral, Justice of the Peace, Judge in the Court of Admiralty, and acting-Governor of Jamaica. He died on 25 August 1688.

Eighteenth-Century Vessels

From the 1750s larger ships began to appear more often, built for the expanding commerce with the colonies. Even so, by 1788 only one in every six vessels was over 200 tons and the coastal and Irish trades were still carried on by small craft of between 20 and 50 tons. The way in which vessels were classified began to change in the late eighteenth century. Until then they had been categorised by the form of the hull, but now they came to be described by the way they were rigged – the configuration of masts and sails. They included, beginning with the smallest: the Sloop (1 mast); Schooner (2 masts); Brig (2 masts); Snow (3 masts); Barque or bark (3 masts); Ship (3 masts).

Some idea of their size may be gathered from the dimensions of the *Endeavour,* the barque in which Captain James Cook made his first voyage to the Pacific from 1768 to 1771: built for the north-east coal trade the vessel was just over 30m long, at the widest part measured about 9m. Vessels owned at Cardiff and Penarth were, of course, much smaller – often referred to as 'sloops' or 'market boats' – and capable of making trips, weather permitting, between Bristol Channel landing-places or to the port of Bristol. Sometimes the owner (helped by a crew of two or three) carried his own goods or, often, goods of several merchants would be carried on one journey. Part-ownership of boats, as an investment, was long-standing practice: in the 1640s Jenkin Tiverton had 'one half quarter of one boat called the *George* of Sully'. A 1655 inventory of the possessions of Morgan Hawkins, a Cardiff smallholder and mariner, listed 'half a quarter share in the *Speedwell'*. John Stacey, a farmer, owned 'one quarter part of a boat called the *Charles* valued at £10'. In the 1690s *Speedwell* (24) belonged to Richard Davies and Nicholas Stedman; Davies also had shares in *Lyon* (20), *Two Brothers* (12) and 'a stone boat'. John Stradling owned (in 1722) a quarter of the *Providence*, but owed £9 for it. Christopher John of Lavernock bought one third of the sloop *Friends Goodwill* for £17 and 10*s*, paying £8 deposit with the balance due in twelve months. The *Cardiff Trade Directory* of 1795 mentions Charles Jones, joint owner and captain of the sloop *Lady of Cardiff*; and Harford, Wetherill and Waters, 'owners of sloops trading from Cardiff to Bristol'.

Although owning ships could be profitable, it could also lead to financial disaster and human tragedy – losses of ship, crew, passengers and cargo were common. Here are a few of the eighteenth-century vessels that came to grief on the dangerous coast of the Vale of Glamorgan:

1712. A French ship, with a cargo of brandy and wine went aground at Sully. A crowd gathered, some armed, and began stealing the cargo, ignoring the customs officer who tried to stop them. A few of the local landowners and their followers arrived to restore order.

1737. The *Pye*, a square-rigged ship, and the brig *Priscilla* were driven on to Nash Point. Hundreds of people ('from all parts of the country towards the hills, particularly from a place called Bridgend') carried away anything moveable.

1752. More looting, this time from the Bristol ship *Indian Prince* (laden with cotton, ebony, ivory, rum and sugar) at Stout Point near Llantwit Major.

1769. *La Concorde* was wrecked at St Donats and the cargo, of rum and brandy, stolen. Several local people were reported to have died from 'overmuch drinking'.

1775. A vessel bringing wheat and flour from South Carolina to Bristol ran aground near Sully. Some of the looted cargo ended up on sale in Bristol, but the ship was saved.

The island of Flat Holm, about five miles from Cardiff, has always been a hazard for shipping and in 1736 sixty soldiers were drowned, a disaster which provided an impetus towards providing a lighthouse on the island. Discussions had been going on for some time between the tenant of Flat Holm, William Crispe, and the Bristol Society of Merchant Venturers, who now agreed to support Crispe's petition to Trinity House asking for permission to build a lighthouse. The petition listed the tolls to be paid to the Merchant Venturers:

> For all Bristol ships to or from foreign parts one-and-a-half pence per ton both inward and outward, according to their reports of tonnage at the custom house, and double these dues on foreign ships. For all coasting vessels to or from Ireland one penny per ton: vessels from St. David's Head or Land's End up the Bristol Channel (market boats excepted) one shilling for every voyage inward and one shilling outward.

Before the compulsory registration of British vessels in 1786 Masters often swore that the tonnage of their vessel was half or two thirds of the real figure, so reducing the sum payable.

The light, which first shone on 1 December 1737, was in an exposed place and the keeper reported after one gale in December 1790 that we expected every moment to be our last. At three o'clock on the morning of the 23rd the tower was struck by lightning. The man attending the fire was knocked down and narrowly escaped falling through the stairway. The iron fire grate was smashed to pieces and the top of the tower considerably damaged.

Two centuries later the lighthouse was automated and the keepers left. It was converted to solar power in 1997.

Cardiff Trade

Large quantities of butter continued to be sent to Bristol and the west of England. In the early years of the seventeenth century this was still a monopoly, which gave its owner the right to transport 3,000 barrels of Welsh butter a year from Welsh ports. This privilege, which could be bought and sold, was held by various speculators over the years, until it was abolished in the 1620s. Agents were employed to buy the butter – at a meeting on 11 May 1639 the Bristol Merchant Venturers appointed Roger Williams and Thomas Young of Newport, together with Robert Ragland, Thomas Kimborne and Richard Jones of Cardiff. Nearly a century later Daniel Defoe wrote of southern Glamorgan that it was 'so well covered with grass and stocked with cattle that they supply the city of Bristol with butter in great quantities salted and barrelled up, just as Suffolk does the city of London'. In 1764 a customs report from Cardiff stressed the role of 'our market boats' in carrying cargoes of oats to Bristol 'and likewise butter and more from hence than from any port in the Channel above or below the Holmes'.

Butter was by no means the only commodity sent out through Cardiff. Others included wool, knitted stockings, flannel, and ringo roots (sea holly) which were sent to the apothecaries of Bristol to be made into medicines and sweets. Bristol's thriving glass industry was a customer for boatloads of kelp, and many cargoes of skins and hides were despatched.

Two of the boats trading regularly with Bristol during the 1660s were *Lyon* (20) and *Speedwell* (24), each making one or two journeys a month. On one typical trip the *Lyon* (Master: Nicholas Brewer) carried 200 bushels of oats, wheat, wool and cloth, hides, household goods, gloves, butter and hops. The *Speedwell* (Master and Merchant: John Brewer) loaded for one voyage: oats, butter, half-a-ton of household goods, beans, bags of stockings, upholstery, old brass, wool, some sheep, a box of hats, returned 'mercerie' and £200 in cash.

On their homeward voyage, boats like *Lyon* and *Speedwell* brought items such as cloth, salt, wine and anything else needed by local households and tradesmen. Passengers were also taken from Cardiff to the West Country and back, and people could go to Bristol on business, to work, or for shopping. A hundred years later the voyages were still going on in the same way – William Thomas of Michaelston refers in his diary to Mr Cadel, a bookseller from Bristol 'to whom I belonged for years to buy books etc'. Edward Williams (1747–1826) – poet, manuscript collector and historian, better known as 'Iolo Morganwg' – was a frequent visitor to Bristol and in the 1770s worked as a stonemason in the west of England, setting up a workshop in Wells in 1783. He went into the transport business by buying a sloop, which sailed between Aberthaw and Bristol, and when he opened his shop in Cowbridge – selling books and general goods – most of his stock was bought from Bristol. As well as the long-established cross-Channel trade in goods and commercial services there was a social and political network and traffic in ideas. Iolo Morganwg had regular contact with radical circles in Bath and Bristol, especially those involved in the anti-slavery movement.

An increasingly popular bulk import to south Wales throughout the eighteenth century was tobacco, often brought in by smugglers along with other items such as brandy and tea. Two tobacco ships are recorded as having anchored in Penarth Roads in September 1648, discharging some of their cargo for Cardiff; two months later the *Lilly* of Bristol landed more tobacco. In the following August the customs officer reported that the *Alice* had arrived from Barbados with 'sugar, cotton, tobacco, fustick wood, and a little ginger'. By 1752 a customs document was able to report that there were eighty to a hundred tobacco shops in and around Cardiff.

Trade was on the increase, Cardiff town quay was rebuilt again in 1762, and the Town Council appointed two water bailiffs 'to supervise the quay and the navigation of the river... and for the preventing of nuisances, such as the leaving of heavy goods on the quay to the hindrance of others, loading and unloading'. If heavy cargo, such as iron or stone, were left for more than twenty-four hours the owners would be fined.

There had also been changes in the customs arrangements. Chepstow was removed from the customs port of Cardiff in 1730, followed by Swansea and Neath in 1735. From the year 1730 no cocket was needed for vessels carrying cargo between places above the Holms, encouraging trade between Cardiff, Newport, Chepstow, Bristol, Gloucester and Tewkesbury, as well as up the Severn Navigation to Worcestershire and Shropshire, although the Cardiff customs officer reported in 1735 that Cardiff was 'the most inconsiderable port for trade' in south Wales and that Chepstow, and Swansea (with Neath) had 'ten times the trade we have'.

William Thomas's diary has a few references to local seamen who ventured far from the Severn Sea. He notes the death in 1762 of Morgan Morgan of Radyr 'on the coast of Guinea,' presumably as a crew member of a slave ship. More than 2,000 slaving voyages were sent out from Bristol during the eighteenth century, organised by agents, of whom at least three may have come from south Wales. Their activities may well have led to the involvement of more Welsh men, as seamen or as investors. William Thomas mentions a handful from around Cardiff – in December 1763 John Morgan ran away to Bristol, to sign on for a voyage to Guinea; John Stephens of Cardiff died on the coast of Guinea serving with Thomas Jones, also of Cardiff. A happier event was the wedding in April 1767 of Thomas Thomas in Cardiff, captain of a Bristol ship employed in the Guinea trade. Another casualty off the Guinea coast was Captain Richard Priest, aged thirty, who was on his third such voyage. Several people from Cardiff had invested in his first venture, but received no dividend and had to take the matter to court. Two brothers, Evan William and William William (of Michaelston-super-Ely) were reported dead in August 1769, having left Bristol in March on a ship bound for Guinea and the West Indies. John Roberts of Cowbridge made thirteen slaving voyages.

There were other ways of going to sea – a press gang came to Cardiff in August 1762 'to clear the prison'. There were also privateering opportunities, such as that reported in *Felix Farley's Bristol Journal* of 1 April 1758: the privateer *Phoenix* had arrived at Bristol 'from a cruise,' and brought in as a prize the *Granard*, a privateer from St Malo. The French vessel, with a crew of over fifty and armed with twelve guns, had been 'out but for four or five days and had taken two colliers from Wales, one of which was bound from Carmarthen to London'. An advertisement in the *Bristol Gazette* of 15 October 1778 sought crew members for the *Hercules*, about to set off on a privateering venture. Men were offered good pay and 'their share of prizes taken'. This was not necessarily a route to riches, but it was rumoured Christopher Basset, brother of the Bonvilston parson, had managed to make £10,000 from such voyages.

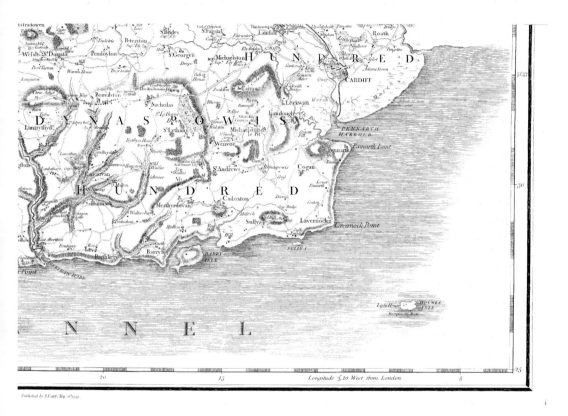

4 Part of George Yates's 1799 'Map of the County of Glamorgan'.

3

THE CANAL PORT

Cardiff's growth as a port went hand-in-hand with industrial developments twenty miles inland. Demand for iron had been increasing from about the 1740s and locally there were forges at Pentyrch, Melingriffith and Cardiff. In the uplands of Glamorgan a coke-fired iron-making furnace had been built at Hirwaun in 1757 and another at Dowlais two years later, the first steps towards what would become a gigantic industry. Cardiff was the link between manufacturers, markets, and sources of raw material to feed the furnaces. Changes in what was produced, how it was produced, and in what quantities had immediate consequences for Cardiff – the port for Merthyr Tydfil.

An important factor in the growth of the south Wales iron industry was the adoption of new manufacturing techniques. In the early days two of the most influential men were Henry Cort of Hampshire and Richard Crawshay of the Cyfarthfa ironworks at Merthyr. The methods of iron-making patented by Henry Cort in 1783–4 resulted in a superior product, and in April 1787 (after thorough trials) the Navy Board ordered 150 tons of iron made by the new process, with the prospect of more contracts to follow. The significance of the Navy's imprimatur was not lost on makers and buyers of iron, and quick off the mark was Richard Crawshay, who signed a contract with Henry Cort on 1 May 1787, agreeing to pay a royalty of 10s a ton on iron made by the new method. Cort supervised the erection of furnaces at Cyfarthfa and taught the local men how to make the iron. Initially, until his own rolling-mill was working, Crawshay's iron had to be shipped from Cardiff to be rolled at either Fontley, near Portsmouth, or at Rotherhithe on the Thames.

Henry Cort's ideas and the ironmasters' initiative had provided the initial impetus, the demand for iron grew, and the south Wales iron industry was now booming. The main cargoes being sent out through Cardiff consisted of merchant bar iron made by the puddling process (using an iron bar to stir the molten iron in the furnace, thus removing carbon). At its destination the iron could have many uses, being made into nails, chains, water-wheels, steam-engines, all sorts of machinery and employed, increasingly, in building.

The great problem for the south Wales ironmasters was that of getting their bulky, weighty product to the customer. The ironworks had been sited near to their raw materials, but the initial stages of transporting the finished articles were frustrating and time-consuming, as they had to be sent down to Cardiff, and from there to merchants in Bristol and London, or to Liverpool for trans-shipment to larger vessels for the

Atlantic crossing. Cargoes could also be sent up the Severn, which was navigable to beyond Shrewsbury, and loads could be carried by canal, via Bewdley, to the towns of the west Midlands and even further afield. At Cardiff, apart from the town quay, iron and other goods might be sent from other shipping places used by 'old established custom' according to a customs report of 1771: Rumney Bridge, 'at the Bank and old quay below Cardiff' and at Leckwith Bridge. Eleven years later another report stated that, 'There are at this port three private wharfs for shipping and landing goods, chiefly iron'.

The laborious trek from Merthyr Tydfil to Cardiff was at first made by horses and mules – in groups of three or four – led by a woman or a boy, and with each animal laden with about a hundredweight (50.8kg) of iron. A turnpike road was built in the early 1770s, which could cope with wagons, each drawn by four horses and carrying up to two tons, but the track soon became worn and full of ruts made by the constant traffic – not only the heavy loads of iron going down to Cardiff, but also the return with everything needed to sustain the ironworks, the employees and their families, and the animals.

Something had to be done, and in May 1787 a Bill was introduced into Parliament with the object of building a canal between Merthyr Tydfil and Cardiff. The Bill became an Act on 9 June 1790, authorising a canal from Merthyr to The Bank, on the River Taff just below Cardiff. The owners were to be *The Company of Proprietors of the Glamorganshire Canal Navigation*, of which most of the shares were taken by the Crawshay family. The contractors Thomas Dadford (senior), Thomas Dadford (junior) and Thomas Sheasby were to build a waterway over 40km long, with a fall from Merthyr to Cardiff of 173m. The canal boats would have to be manoeuvred through fifty-one locks (between Abercynon and Quakers Yard there were sixteen locks within 1.6km) and the waterway was to be 9m wide and 1.2m deep. The Taff had to be spanned by an aqueduct at Abercynon, and there was a tunnel over 100m long at Cardiff.

By 1 October 1790 John Bird was able to inform his employer, the Marquess of Bute, that 'the canal goes on rapidly' and on 2 May 1792: 'Iron is now brought down the Canal from Merthyr to within half a mile of Newbridge'(Pontypridd). On 17 August 1793 the judge for the Great Sessions to be held at Cardiff, Judge Hardinge, 'came from Merthyr to Newbridge in one of the canal boats, accompanied by Mr. Samuel Homfray, with a harper'. The culmination came on 10 February 1794, when a flotilla of canal boats arrived at Cardiff 'laden with the produce of the iron-works... to the great joy of the whole town'. The boats used on the canal were horse-drawn, 18.3m long and 2.7m wide, carrying a usual load of about 20 tons.

Two years later another Act of Parliament permitted an extension of the canal 'to a place called Lower Layer'. On the southern side of Cardiff a mile-long canal basin was built, together with a sea lock, so that ships could be moved between sea and canal. John Bird noted, on 27 February 1798 that, 'The Canal is now ready to admit brigs etc, but the iron is not yet moved to the Canal Wharfs and Basin near the South Gate'. The basin was able to take ships of up to 150 tons, although most of those using it were smaller.

At Cardiff the iron was transferred to a sea-going vessel. The larger ships in British waters at this time were of about 300 tons but, of the 9,000 or so vessels owned in British ports, over 80 per cent were of less than 200 tons. Small craft of 20 to 50 tons still carried most of the trade around the coast, to Ireland, and across the English Channel. Some of those belonging to local owners were given names such as *Partridge, Lady Cardiff, Heart of Oak, Zephyr, Lynn, Draper, Sarah, Jenny* and *Lady Valletort*. Sloops plying

(1031)

ANNO TRICESIMO SEXTO

Georgii III. Regis.

●∗∗∗●

CAP. LXIX.

An Act to amend an Act of the Thirtieth Year of
His present Majefty, for making and maintaining a
Navigable Canal from *Merthyr Tidvile*, to and
through a Place called *The Bank*, near the Town
of *Cardiff*, in the County of *Glamorgan*, and for
extending the faid Canal to a Place called *The
Lower Layer*, below the faid Town.
                                    [26th *April* 1796.]

HEREAS an Act of Parliament was made in the Thir- Preamble,
tieth Year of the Reign of His prefent Majefty, for recites Act
making and maintaining a Navigable Canal from *Merthyr* Cap. 82.
Tidvile, to and through a Place called *The Bank*, near
the Town of *Cardiff*, in the County of *Glamorgan*, and
by the faid Act feveral Perfons are united and made
One Body Politick and Corporate, by the Name of *The Company of
Proprietors of the Glamorganſhire Canal Navigation*, and are authorifed
to make the faid Canal, with the feveral Works relating thereto, and to
raife any Sum of Money for defraying the Expences thereof, not ex-
ceeding Ninety thoufand Pounds: And whereas the faid Company of
Proprietors have raifed the faid Sum of Ninety thoufand Pounds, and
the fame hath been expended in carrying on the faid Canal and other
                    12 E 2   Works,

5 *Above:* A canal boat at Trallwn
Wharf, Pontypridd. During the
late nineteenth century there was
a regular service of market boats
from Cardiff.

6 *Left:* The Act of Parliament
of 1796, which permitted the
extension of the Glamorganshire
Canal to 'The Lower Layer'.

between Cardiff and Bristol were owned by James Walters, who added the *Cardiff Castle* to his fleet in the summer of 1790. In the following year his vessels were bought by William Taitt, the Dowlais ironmaster, who was trying to gain a measure of control over the Dowlais supply route from Bristol.

In April 1791 John Bird reported the launch of a Cardiff-built vessel: 'Mr. Blannin's brig launched this afternoon, raised upon the stocks and immediately loaded with iron for London. Owing to the neglect of the ship's carpenters in leaving a port hole open the vessel filled in the night and sank, but was freed the next day. A man who lay aboard was nearly drowned'.

By the 1830s railroad enterprises were becoming the most important customers, and in 1848 half of all iron produced was being used to provide rails for the new British railway enterprises. When home demand began to wane it was offset by the huge orders from overseas and by the 1850s the ironworks of south Wales dominated this market. An increasing flow of products and raw materials was now being handled at Cardiff.

There had, over the years, been developments in the land transport serving the port as pack-animals had given way to carts, which had in turn been replaced by canal boats. In 1812 the Aberdare Canal had opened, joining the Glamorganshire at Abercynon, and encouraging the growth of the iron industry in the Cynon valley. Although the Glamorganshire Canal had enabled the ironworks to expand output, and facilitated the import of raw materials, the waterway was far from trouble-free. On 8 December 1794 the Canal Company reported that there was a breach in the canal, and could not say when it might be navigable again. A dry summer could cause difficulties, and in August 1800 John Bird wrote to the Marquess of Bute that: 'Owing to the dryness of the season, little or no trade has been done on the Canal from want of water.' Leaking dock walls had to be rebuilt, for example in the summer of 1841 when the locks at Aberfan were closed for three weeks and cargoes had to be unloaded and trundled to the other side of the obstruction, there to be loaded on to another boat. Boats themselves might become an obstacle by being left unattended in an awkward spot, or by sinking. The canal was the equivalent of a modern motorway between Merthyr Tydfil (by now the largest town in Wales, with a population of 35,000) and Cardiff (the population had grown to 10,000 by 1841) – any interruption in the flow of traffic was a serious matter. By the 1820s and 1830s over 200 craft were using the waterway, which was becoming overwhelmed. Sunday working had been introduced and locks, tunnel, and sea lock were all lit by lamps so that boats could work throughout the night.

Traffic problems were at their worst below Abercynon where, from 1802, a tram road joined the canal bringing the output of the Dowlais, Penydarren and Plymouth works. Horses pulled trains of trams down to the canal wharf, using the track on which, on 21 February 1804, Richard Trevithick's steam locomotive demonstrated that it was possible to haul a load of iron, and people, on smooth rails.

The *Cardiff and Merthyr Guardian* published the statistics of iron sent down the canal in the year 1834:

William Crawshay and Sons (Cyfarthfa) 34,000 tons
Dowlais Iron Company 33,000
Penydarren Ironworks 12,000
Hill's Plymouth Works 12,000

7 The Glamorganshire Canal at Abercynon. Between Abercynon and Quaker's Yard boats had to negotiate sixteen locks in 1.6km – an inevitable source of delays.

Melingriffith Works 3,000
Brown Lenox 1,000
Other works 15,000
Total: 110,000 tons.

The canal was built, primarily, to take cargoes to and from the ironworks, but many other items were carried, including the great variety of commodities needed by the expanding town of Merthyr, as well as tinplate from Melingriffith and the output of the Ynysangharad (Pontypridd) chain works. The works had been owned by the Tappendens of Abernant Ironworks, but was taken over in 1818 by Captain Samuel Brown, who had formed a partnership with his cousin Samuel Lenox to make chain cables for use in ships. Brown and Lenox supplied their cables to warships such as *Dreadnought*, *Hood* and *Rodney* and to merchant vessels including Brunel's *Great Eastern* and the Cunarders *Aquitania* and *Mauretania*. The firm was also involved in building suspension bridges, including the Union Bridge of 1819–20 near Berwick-upon-Tweed. Further down the waterway at Nantgarw, china-making began in the 1790s, and from 1813 to 1822 a famous, but luxury, product was the porcelain made by William Billingsley and Samuel Walker. Up the canal came bone, sand, potash, china clay and down went Billingsley's delicate wares. Later on, the cargoes sent to Cardiff from Nantgarw consisted of clay tobacco pipes from what had now become 'The Old China Works'.

A New Market for Coal

Advances were being made in maritime technology and a few steam-powered boats appeared in the Bristol Channel. In the early 1820s steam packet services were inaugurated from Bristol to Chepstow, Newport and Swansea. Steam boats were employed at the Old and New Passages across the Severn from 1827 and a service between Bristol and Cardiff was started in 1834.

All the steamships were propelled by paddle wheels, and their crews had to cope with the difficulty of the variable immersion of the wheels – if the ship rolled to port then part of the starboard wheel lifted out of the water, while the port one went in deeper. Immersion to other than the optimum depth could also be caused by changes in the weight being carried, whether of coal, cargo, or the number of passengers. It was thought that paddle boats were best suited to conveying passengers on fairly short voyages in sheltered waters, and as tug boats, manoeuvering sailing ships into, around, and out of, a port (although the paddler *Great Western* began to operate from Bristol to New York in 1838, with a maiden voyage of fifteen days and five hours). Attempts were made to overcome the paddlers' operating deficiencies by using another method of propulsion – a screw propeller at the stern – and a pioneer of this new idea appeared off Cardiff in May 1840. The *Archimedes*, originally called the *Propeller*, was launched in 1839 with a screw 1.7m in diameter driving a vessel of 200 tons and 38m in length. *Archimedes* set off on a promotional trip around Britain, visiting Bristol in May 1840, and demonstrating her capabilities by taking passengers on an excursion to Steep Holm and Flat Holm. The new craft impressed Brunel, who recommended the adoption of screw propulsion for the *Great Britain*, which was being built at Bristol.

Developments in the design of steam vessels, and their greater numbers, would lead to an increased demand for coal from south Wales. The Cardiff Port Books show that occasional cargoes of coal were being sent from Cardiff to La Rochelle in the 1590s, but by 1775 a customs official felt able to report that, '... no coal can be ever raised within this port in order to be shipped for exportation or to be carried coastwise, its distance from the water rendering it too expensive for any sale.' Seven years later another customs report stated that, 'we have no coals exported from this port, nor ever shall, as it would be too expensive to bring it down here from the internal part of the country'.

The sale of coal from Cardiff was not encouraged by the fact that coal shipped through some other ports was exempt from the coastwise duty if 'carried on the Monmouthshire Canal or railways connected therewith' and then conveyed on the Severn 'from any place to the eastward of the Holms... to any other place in or upon the River Severn also to the eastward of the Holms'. (*House of Lords Journal*. Vol. 62, 1830). Newport, Bristol and Bridgwater all benefited from this arrangement, as may be seen from the statistics for 1829: coal shipped to Bristol from Newport 94,968 tons, from Cardiff 10 tons. Coal shipped to Bridgwater from Newport 79,846 tons, from Cardiff nil. Some coal was sent down the Glamorganshire Canal to Cardiff, in the 1790s for example from Thomas Key's colliery at Abercanaid, but the quantity of coal going out through Cardiff was a good deal less than at Newport. In 1829 Newport exported a total of 472,888 tons, Cardiff 57,829 tons (70 per cent to Ireland, 30 per cent to other ports in Great Britain) and Swansea 20,401 tons. On 12 June 1830 Walter Coffin 'of Llandaff Court, Glamorganshire' appeared before the House of Lords Select Committee on the coal trade. He had been involved in the business at Cardiff for twenty years and told the committee that nearly all of his coal was sent to Ireland, especially to Cork and Waterford. Most of the coal came from Newport – 'we are sending very little from Cardiff now'. Coffin's vessels also went to Barnstaple, Bideford and to some ports in Cornwall. He told the Committee that, 'The ships employed in the coal trade are generally employed in the coal trade all the year round, but there are other ships which are employed in the corn trade or other trades which, when not so employed, get into the coal trade as a last resource.'

The Monmouthshire Canal's (and Newport's) tax concession was abolished in 1831, to be followed by a big increase in Cardiff's coal trade: at the start of the decade just over 100,000 tons were brought down the Glamorganshire Canal – by 1840 this had reached around 200,000 tons, with the trade being conducted through local merchants such as Walter Coffin, George Insole, Morgan Thomas, Lucy Thomas, John Edmonds, Duncan & Co. and Thomas Powell. In 1830 Powell took a lease on a wharf at the sea lock, put down a tram road to a jetty on the Taff, and so was able to load or discharge cargo on the river as well as on the canal.

The partnership of Insole and Biddle had a coal yard (as well as a dry dock) at Cardiff, and also owned a brickyard. The usual way of selling coal was direct to ships' masters who turned up at the dockside but Insole's aim was to acquire long-term contracts and, as well as supplying the local steamship companies, he was soon shipping large quantities (100 tons a day by 1834) to the tugs and passenger vessels on the Thames. The business was not confined to the British Isles and George Insole's customers could be found in Brest, Nantes, Calais and Marseille. John Nixon was another who took his wares to Nantes, where he demonstrated Welsh coal to such effect that the sugar refineries gave up using Newcastle coal and contracted with Nixon, who also won orders from the operators of river steamers and from the French government. By the late 1840s Walter Coffin was also exporting coal to Nantes, often six shiploads a week.

Imports of iron ore had also increased. By the 1820s, ore-carrying vessels came to Cardiff from the Forest of Dean and the south-west of England (from such ports as Plymouth, Wadebridge and Fowey) but the bulk of the supplies came from Furness and Cumberland, with ships loading at Barrow-in-Furness, Ulverston and Whitehaven. By the middle of the century south Wales ironmasters were relying on these sources of ore and, to make certain of supplies, took control of many of the mines.

With this growth in the coal and iron ore trade the number of ships visiting Cardiff increased from 1,109 vessels in 1826 to 2,822 in 1835. Their numbers also included those small sailing craft which provided regular services – to and from Bridgwater went *Friends* (master, John Davy) and *Venus* (John Gilleford); to Bristol *Amity* (David Rogers), *Brothers* (Thomas Rosser), *Castle* (David Walters), *Ebenezer* (Thomas Thomas), *Friends* (Daniel Vaughan) and *Merthyr Packet* (James Phillips). Those voyaging to London were *Cambria* (William Pettigrew), *Cardiff Packet* (Benjamin Harvey), *Glamorgan* (William Hughes) and *Memnon* (Samuel Phillips).

The increase in the number of vessels wanting to load or unload cargo made the sea lock of the Glamorganshire Canal a constant source of delay and frustration and the situation was often chaotic. The basin was lengthened in 1814, but problems persisted as it was silting up, a situation not helped by the practice of dumping ballast into the water. Vessels were almost 'grid-locked'. Those of about 70 tons were loaded in the upper part of the basin – nearest to Cardiff – where the water was about 2.4m deep; larger vessels (of 100 to 150 tons) were moored at the lower end, in about 4.6m of water.

8 *Right:* Discharging coal at Rotherhithe. By the 1830s steamboat companies on the Thames were receiving regular supplies from Cardiff.

9 *Below:* The Glamorganshire Canal wharves at Cardiff, crossed by the Great Western Railway line. The first building on the left is the Custom House, built in about 1845.

10 A view of Cardiff around 1840. The conical structures in the middle distance are part of the Glass Works, towards the seaward end of the canal basin. Mount Stuart Square was built on the site.

There was a constant shuffling about, and when a ship in the part nearest the town had taken on about two thirds of its cargo it had to be moved into deeper water further down the wharf to finish loading.

Many vessels were too big to enter the sea lock and had to anchor out in the bay, where their cargo was dealt with by lighters. Just getting to the sea lock was hazardous because the channel from Penarth Roads was narrow and winding and it was easy for vessels to become stuck, which could mean being stranded there for days.

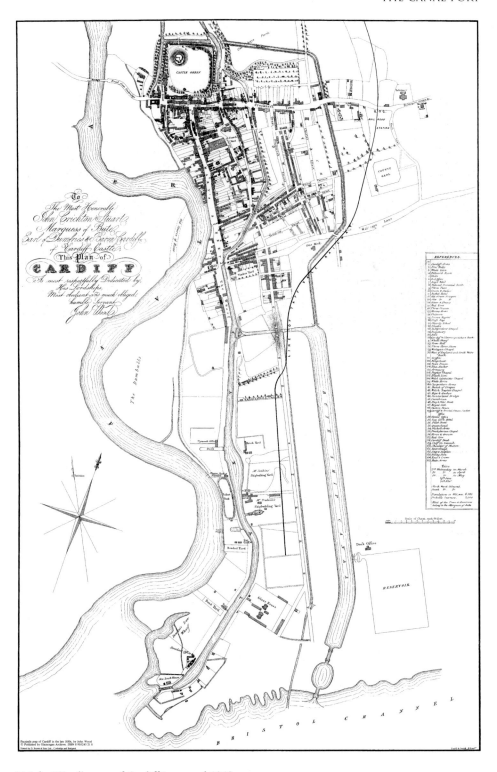

11 John Wood's map of Cardiff in around 1840.

4

HIS LORDSHIP'S DOCKS

The Glamorganshire Canal proprietors decided that something had to be done about their overloaded waterway and commissioned George Overton to report on the situation at Cardiff. Overton (a partner in various coal-mining enterprises and the ironworks at Hirwaun, as well as being an engineer) came up with suggestions for the improvement of that part of the canal between the sea lock and the wharves. It should be made straighter and deeper, and a new basin was needed. The canal owners wanted something done but found that most of their proposals were stymied by the Marquess of Bute, whose land kept the canal company's operations hemmed in.

The 2nd Marquess of Bute was in his late twenties at this time and came to Cardiff, usually, twice a year. Partially-sighted, he had problems with reading and writing but this did not prevent him from taking a close interest in the administration of his vast estates. Having been reluctant to sanction any development of the Canal Company's facilities, the Bute advisers were now weighing up the possibilities of undertaking such work for the benefit of his lordship.

An experienced canal engineer, James Green, was asked for his opinion. He was, of course, not impressed by the tortuous approach-channel from the sea or by the scrum of vessels at high tide trying to get in or out of the sea lock. James Green proposed to do away with the winding approach by constructing a ship canal, 2.4km long, from the sea to East Moors. From this canal vessels would enter a new dock, which would be connected to the Glamorganshire Canal so that boats could be moved between canal and dock for the trans-shipment of cargoes. Green's ideas were embodied in a Parliamentary Bill, which was opposed by the owners of the Melingriffith tinplate works (who thought that their water supply might be affected) and by the Monmouthshire and Glamorganshire Canal Companies. In spite of this opposition the Act came into force on 16 July 1830.

The project could now go ahead, but the Marquess of Bute delayed, taking further advice before committing himself to such an expensive scheme. William Cubbitt suggested that, instead of building an entrance canal, there should be a dredged channel – a much cheaper option, which received the approval of Parliament in May 1834.

Construction began. A new weir was thrown across the Taff and work was put in hand on the dock feeder canal through the town centre. The new dredged channel (or 'mud cut') which brought ships up to the dock was just over 1,200m long. Having negotiated this, vessels fetched up in a basin before entering the dock itself, which was 1,219m long and 61m wide.

11 GEO. IV. --Sess. 1830.

A

B I L L

For empowering the Most Honourable *John Crichton Stuart* Marquis of *Bute* and Earl of *Dumfries*, to make and maintain a Ship Canal, to commence at a certain place called *The Eastern Hollows*, near the Mouth of the River *Taff*, in the County of *Glamorgan*, and to terminate near the Town of *Cardiff*, in the said County, with other Works to communicate therewith.

WHEREAS the making and maintaining a Ship Canal, to commence at a certain point or place called *The Eastern Hollows*, at or near the mouth of the River *Taff*, in the County of *Glamorgan*, and to terminate in a northern or north-easterly direction towards the Town of *Cardiff*, in *Cardiff* Moors; and also the establishing and constructing a Wet Dock or Basin and other Works, at the termination of the said Ship Canal, near the said Town of *Cardiff*; and also the making and maintaining ~~one or more~~ Cuts or Canals out of and from the said Wet Dock or Basin, to communicate with the *Glamorganshire* Canal, together with Sluices or Tunnels, Piers and other Works joining and communicating with the said Ship Canal, Wet Dock or Basin, Cuts or Canals and other Works, will, by avoiding the dangers and difficulties of the present intricate Navigation from the Sea to the said *Glamorganshire* Canal, and by affording additional accommodation and security

Preamble.
Expediency of forming a Ship Canal, Wet Dock, and other Works.

40.   A   to

[handwritten note:] + The intended cuts to communicate with the Glamorganshire Canal will, (as admitted in the Preamble,) be the means of avoiding the dangers &c of the present intricate Navigation & will be of great advantage to the Public in general. — Will not these Cuts be of much greater advantage & if Lord Bute's intentions are to accommodate the Public, why not make these Cuts &.

12 The Bute Ship Canal Bill 1830. This enabled the Marquess of Bute, after an Amending Act of 1834, to build his first dock – later known as the West Bute Dock – which opened in 1839.

The official inauguration was on 9 October 1839 when the paddler *Lady Charlotte* (75) – owned by the Bristol Steam Navigation Company – brought in the *Celerity*, a local schooner with the civic party on board. On 25 October the first foreign vessel arrived when the *Warsaw* of New York was towed in by the wooden paddle-steamer *Nautilus.* Unfortunately, the dock had to be closed in the following spring because of construction faults, and was not completely operational for another six months.

As work began on the new Bute dock, a new railroad was being planned. The idea of a Taff Vale Railway was most strongly supported by those Merthyr ironmasters who were fed up with the Crawshay-controlled Glamorganshire Canal, and who felt that a more efficient transport system to Cardiff would increase their profits. Isambard Kingdom Brunel was commissioned to survey a possible route and reported in February 1835. A meeting on 12 October of that year at the Castle Inn, Merthyr – chaired by John Josiah Guest of Dowlais and attended by other ironmasters – decided to promote a Bill, which received the royal assent on 21 June 1836.

The first section of the railway line, from Cardiff to Abercynon, opened on 9 October 1840 (one year after the new Bute Dock) with the shareholders travelling in a special train to Cardiff, where they dined at the Cardiff Arms Hotel. The whole line to Merthyr Tydfil – 39.4km – opened on 12 April 1841.

The TVR's intention, as stated in the 1836 Act, was to build a dock at Cogan Pill, near Penarth. This was obviously not in the interests of Lord Bute and his dock, and after long and convoluted negotiations an agreement was arrived at in 1844 which meant that the railway's owners could avoid the expense of building their own port. The east side of the Bute dock would be leased to the TVR for 250 years, on condition that the railway proprietors abandoned their proposal for a rival dock. These provisions became law by Act of Parliament on 26 August 1846. The TVR decided that its new railway into the Bute Docks would be elevated, so that a new kind of tipping machinery could be used – a coal wagon was shunted into the top part of the tipper and then hydraulically tilted, allowing the coal to fall down a chute into the ship's hold.

In June 1850 trains of the South Wales Railway began to serve Cardiff, where building the new railway station meant moving the River Taff. The river was diverted along a new channel, away from the quay, which was later to be buried under the new Westgate Street. As well as having the river moved, the managers of this new railway wanted easy access to the Bute Dock but this, although only a dozen years old, was already too crowded.

The foundations for Cardiff's future as a coal port had been laid:

A large dock had been built by the Marquess of Bute.

The opening of the Taff Vale Railway encouraged the development of coal-mining in the port's hinterland. The main line opened in 1841, trains ran into the Cynon valley from 1846 and the Rhondda branch began operating in the mid-1850s.

There was growing demand for coal to fuel steam boilers, including those of ships, and the collieries served by the Cardiff Docks happened to mine the best steam coal.

A scientific experiment would publicise the advantages of south Wales coal for raising steam.

13 The source of Cardiff's prosperity.

The Growing Demand for Steam Coal

The increasing numbers of steamships provided a large potential market for coal. In 1839 there were about 21,000 sailing ships and only 723 steam ships. By 1890 there were 7,400 steamers, about one third of all ships registered in Britain.

Opportunities to sell steam coal to London multiplied – by the 1840s the General Steam Navigation Company's fleet on the Thames had grown to nearly fifty, with vessels providing regular services between places such as Gravesend, Greenwich and Woolwich. Long-distance steam-powered services were encouraged by mail contracts and in 1837 the forerunner of the P&O Line contracted for a monthly voyage to Gibraltar and, later, to Egypt, India and Hong Kong. Cunard began services across the Atlantic, and Royal Mail Lines to the West Indies.

This expansion of steamer services led to the stockpiling of coal along the regular routes, at places such as Aden – until the Suez Canal opened in 1869 P&O sent regular cargoes of Welsh steam there, via the Cape of Good Hope. Ship-owners signed annual contracts for this bunker coal and by the end of the nineteenth century Port Said was taking in well over 1 million tons a year, as were Las Palmas and Montevideo. Prominent in the provision of coal at steamer bunkering stops was the firm of Cory Brothers which sent coal all over the world. By the early 1900s they had over a hundred depots or agencies in places like Aden, Algiers, Bahia Blanca, Barbados, Buenos Aires, Cape Verde Islands, Las Palmas, Marseille, Pernambuco, Port Said and Rio de Janeiro. In 1913, 36 million tons of British coal were exported for use by steamships, over half of the country's total coal exports.

The operation of coaling a ship at one of these bunkering stops was likely to be tedious, time-consuming, and dirty – with coal dust finding every crevice of the ship. A typical scene in many places would be of hundreds of local people, with baskets full of coal on their heads, negotiating planks connecting a barge, or wharf, to the ship.

Coal Trials

Two benefactors of the south Wales coal trade turned out to be Sir Henry de la Beche and Dr Lyon Playfair. Beche was a well-known geologist, who became the first director

14 Coaling ship at St Lucia.

15 Dr Lyon Playfair. With Henry de la Beche he supervised the trials to find the best coal for use by vessels of the Royal Navy. The results, favouring Welsh coal, gave a timely boost to the south Wales industry.

of the Geological Survey of Great Britain in 1835. Lyon Playfair was also a scientist, as well as being a Member of Parliament, Postmaster-General and, later, the 1st Baron Playfair of St Andrews. As more and more steamships came on the scene, their operators wanted to know if there was any difference in the effectiveness of the various kinds of coal being offered to them. The Admiralty decided to finance trials, to be supervised by de la Beche and Playfair. Nearly 100 kinds of coal were examined, more than a third of them from south Wales, and each type was tested for such factors as evaporation characteristics, weight of a cubic foot of coal, and the space occupied by 1 ton. The results, published as *Reports on the Coals suited for the Steam Navy* (1848, 1849 and 1851), showed that the Welsh coals were generally better than the others – they caught light more easily, made steam quickly, left little clinker, and produced less smoke.

These results were of enormous significance for south Wales. Regular orders for coal came from the Royal Navy and all steamship companies followed this lead. Coal exports from Cardiff rocketed, growing from 200,000 tons a year in 1843 to 750,000 tons a year by the 1850s.

The East Bute Dock

By the early 1850s ships were queuing to get a berth in the Bute Dock and the larger vessels now coming into service could not get in at all. A report from John Plews and Sir John Rennie in July 1847 recommended that a new dock was needed. The 2nd

Marquess died in the following year, to be succeeded by his infant son, which meant that the management of the estates was put into the hands of trustees, who had to grapple with a decision about a new dock. The trustees were obliged to be cautious about spending the infant Marquess's money, as did Parliament, which gave final approval for any major expenditure. There were good reasons why the Bute estate should not build one, because the return on the investment in the existing dock was low, and a new dock was likely to suck in more and more money as time went on. Yet there were reasons for building a new dock: if the congestion was not eased trade would diminish, leading to financial losses, whereas spending money now might keep the whole enterprise in profit. It was decided to go ahead, with the original dock becoming known as the West Bute Dock and the new one the East Bute Dock.

The dock now built was 1,310m long, 91m wide for a quarter of its length and 152m wide for the remainder. It was 7.6m deep. The first part of the dock opened on 20 July 1855, when the tug *Queen* towed in the Sunderland barque *William Jones*, dressed overall and with yards manned. Four other vessels followed, and then Francis Crawshay's yacht, to the music of his Cyfarthfa Iron Works band.

A tidal harbour with four balance-tipping machines opened in 1856, for use by small coasting vessels, and by 1857 in one month alone nearly 350 vessels left Cardiff for foreign ports. There was frenetic competition at the docks as ship-brokers and others kept a twenty-four-hour look-out, and hustled for business with arriving vessels. (A ship-broker acted as agent for a visiting vessel's master, dealing with the necessary documentation, paying port dues and customs duties. He could also order stores, supply crew members, find a cargo, and arrange the charter, sale or purchase of vessels.) Fights were known to break out between competitors in what was a lucrative, booming market.

The nature of the ships arriving at Cardiff was changing. By the end of the 1850s most British steam ships were of iron and new vessels were, usually, fitted with iron screw-propellers. An iron vessel lasted longer, was cheaper to build and maintain, and could carry more cargo than a similar wooden vessel.

The first iron screw collier was the *John Bowes,* launched by the Palmer Brothers' yard at Jarrow on 30 June 1852. The vessel could carry 650 tons of coal, and made the round trip from the Tyne to London, including loading and unloading, in under five days. It took two brigs a month to do the same job. In south Wales Thomas Powell took delivery in 1856 of the *Thomas Powell* (401) – an iron, screw-propelled steamer built at Bristol – and in the following year *The Times* (16 July 1857) announced that the *William Cory* would soon be starting regular voyages between Cardiff and London. The vessel was owned by William Cory and John Nixon, a partnership which was in the process of buying Deep Duffryn Colliery at Mountain Ash. Newly built by Charles Mitchell's yard on the Tyne, *William Cory* (1,578) could carry 1,500 tons of coal – over twice as much as the *John Bowes* – and was able to use water as ballast on the return trip. At first the *William Cory* was unloaded at Victoria Dock in London, but the owners later switched to a hulk called *Great Atlas* moored off Angerstein Wharf where hydraulic cranes discharged the coal on to one side of the hulk and loaded it into lighters on the other side. Much of *William Cory*'s subsequent career was as a cable-laying ship, being chartered first by Glass Elliot & Co. of Greenwich and then by the Telegraph Construction and Maintenance Company. Telegraph cables laid included: 1858 Suffolk to Holland, and Cromer to Emden; 1859 Cromer to Heligoland; 1861 Algiers to Toulon, and Otranto to Corfu; 1866 the Irish

Transatlantic cable. Valentia 1866

16 The *William Cory*, owned by William Cory and John Nixon, was a purpose-built collier which began taking coal from Cardiff to London in 1857. A year later it began a career as a cable-laying vessel. Its role in laying the Irish end of the transatlantic cable was commemorated by this Irish postage stamp of 1979.

coast end of the Atlantic cable; 1869 the French Atlantic cable. During 1870 the *William Cory* was working in the Red Sea and the Mediterranean.

The second part of the East Dock opened on 19 January 1858 and the final section was declared open on 14 September 1859 by the 3rd Marquess of Bute (aged twelve) and his mother, who were on board the steam tug *United States* – owned by the Bute Dock Steam Towing Company – which brought in the barque *Masaniello* (perhaps an inappropriately named vessel to open a marquess's dock – Masaniello was a Neapolitan who led a revolt against the nobility). The celebrations were muted because of the recent death of Lord James Stuart, the young Lord Bute's uncle. The *Illustrated London News* wrote (1 October 1859) that 'the intended festivities were dispensed with, and the dock was opened for trade in the quietest possible manner'. The *Cardiff and Merthyr Guardian* noted that only a few people turned up, 'who, having heard of the intended formal opening, had hastened to the spot'. The newspaper went on to report that, at the same time as the *United States* and *Masaniello* entered the dock, 'the new canal, which forms a junction with the Bute West Dock and the Glamorgan Ship Canal, was opened by one of the Aberdare Coal Company's boats (No.267), with a cargo of coal for Messrs. David and Toms, and an empty lighter passing through the locks. With the exception of a small steamer belonging to the contractors for the works, Messrs. Hemingway and Co, which followed the *Masaniello* with a small party, this constituted the whole of the opening of the extension'.

As the docks grew, so did the dangers. Men often fell into the water, and there were thefts from warehouses, vessels and seamen. Machines were a constant hazard and people were injured or killed by railway and coaling operations. Drunkenness and fights

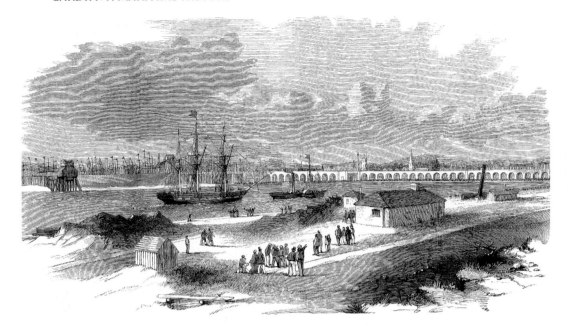

17 The opening of the final part of the East Bute Dock on 14 September 1859. The twelve-year-old Marquess of Bute and his mother were on board the tug *United States*, towing the barque *Masaniello*.

– between individuals and between groups – became commonplace, often with the use of knuckle-dusters, knives, or even guns. Bare-knuckle contests were held on the East Moors. W.J. Trounce, who worked in a shipping office at the docks, described how 'there were many low-class dancing rooms in Bute Street... Many disturbances occurred at these places, giving much trouble to the police and bringing considerable notoriety to the town'. The town's small number of policemen could not cope, pressure was put on the dock managers, and the Bute Docks Police Force was formed towards the end of the 1850s, with the men dressed in green serge uniforms and armed with cutlasses. (The Force continued until 1922, when the eighty men were absorbed into the Great Western Railway Police.)

1868 was another active year for the Bute trustees: coal staithes were built on the Taff's east bank, and the new Low Water Pier was inaugurated. This (427m long and 10.4m wide) was for passenger steamers, and supported rail and carriage ways, as well as waiting rooms. The Roath Basin opened for business on 25 July 1874. Built on the site of the Bute Tidal Harbour, it was designed as an entrance to a bigger dock.

Iron

In the mid-1850s came an innovation which was to affect the whole iron industry. Henry Bessemer's process produced a metal that was cheaper and quicker to make than wrought iron, but could be used for the same purposes. Cold air was blown through molten cast iron in a converter to produce Bessemer steel, later known as 'mild steel'.

18 Plan of Cardiff and Penarth, 1869.

19 Roath Basin under construction in 1872. It opened for business on 25 July 1874.

The total output of wrought iron was not at first affected, but declined around the 1870s, and the closure of Glamorgan ironworks began. Cyfarthfa shut down in 1872, but re-opened to make steel in 1882. (Closed again eighteen years later, it operated once more for four years during the First World War, before final closure in 1919.) The Dowlais Works, where 8,000 people were employed, took out the first licence to make Bessemer's steel.

Bessemer's process, to work properly, needed an iron ore with a low phosphorus content. It could be found in Vizcaya, northern Spain, where considerable open-cast mining began, mainly financed from Britain. From the 1860s new railways, built with British capital, linked the mines with the port of Bilbao and soon 75 per cent of the output was being shipped to the British Isles. Spain had become a major importer of Welsh coal, which meant that ships could now return to Cardiff carrying ore, rather than ballast. The Dowlais Company, the Consett Iron Company (of County Durham) and Krupp (of Germany) formed the Orconera Iron Company of Bilbao to make certain of their ore supplies, and firms such as the Bilbao Iron Ore Company opened offices in Cardiff.

Having shipped the ore to Cardiff, the Dowlais Company now had to transport it 40km inland to the ironworks, and then send finished steel back down to Cardiff for export, so in 1888 the company began to build 'Dowlais-by-the-Sea,' a new works next to Cardiff Docks. The first iron was made there in 1891, with the steel works and plating mill starting production four years later.

Until the late 1850s most iron products still came to Cardiff by the Glamorganshire Canal. The volume of traffic diminished in the 1870s, with the decline of the ironworks, although it was thought worthwhile to make some improvements to the canal, and in the early 1870s the sea lock basin was enlarged and made deeper.

The docks were overcrowded again by the 1880s, with the familiar delays for cargoes and ships. The *Bute Docks Act* (1882) authorised the Roath Dock, which was to be built on reclaimed land. Work started in 1883 and the *Cardiff Times* of 3 January described 'The turning of the first sod of the new docks which the Marquis of Bute is constructing in close proximity to the existing dock system, which has helped in such a material way to

20 Bilbao in 1862. A new railway connects the port to the iron-mining areas. Bilbao was to become a familiar destination for Cardiff seamen, whose ships made regular deliveries of Welsh coal and returned with cargoes of iron ore.

21 The mud cut – the approach to Cardiff Docks in 1872.

make Cardiff what it is'. Lord Bute arrived by railway train and inaugurated the work by starting a steam-driven digger. There was a long and varied procession, with several bands, and luncheon and speeches. The same issue of the *Cardiff Times* reported that 'A new dry dock is being constructed by Messrs. Morel at the south-east corner of the Roath Basin.' While the Roath Dock was being built it was decided to incorporate the Marquess's docks as a public company, to be called *The Bute Docks Company*.

Coal

In the 1840s there had been only a handful of coal sales agencies. A local business directory for 1859 lists forty 'coal owners and coal merchants' with offices in Cardiff, including Walter Coffin (Bute Docks), George Insole and Son (Bute Crescent), John Nixon (West Bute Street) and Thomas Powell (Bute Street). By 1913 the number had grown to seventy-four. Until 1886 most of the inevitable haggling over coal contracts was done in the open air, a situation that was to be remedied by Frederick de Courcy Hamilton, a local solicitor. Hamilton had seen the coal trading going on out-of-doors, often in Mount Stuart Square. Borrowing a large sum of money, he intended 'to give the docksmen shelter', taking a lease on land in the middle of the square – on ground occupied many years before by the Cardiff glassworks – to erect his Exchange building. As architect he employed Edwin Seward, who was also responsible for Cardiff Free Library in The Hayes, the Royal Infirmary and Penarth's Turner House art gallery. Hamilton inaugurated an Exchange Club for coal traders – only members were allowed on to the trading floor, which was open for an hour a day. The *Coal Exchange*, a private business enterprise of Hamilton's, opened for trading on 1 February 1886 and soon established itself as the hub of the Welsh – and world – coal trade.

Roath Dock, declared open on 24 August 1887, was fitted out with up-to-date equipment, including the new Lewis-Hunter cranes, which were designed to avoid breaking the coal as it was dropped into a ship's hold. The cranes could be moved along

22 An engraving of 'The Docks, Cardiff'.

23 The West Dock.

the dock, and three or more could be used simultaneously on one vessel, loading a cargo of 10,000 tons of coal in twenty-four hours. The Dowlais Company took over 300m of the quay for iron imports and steel exports, and 'lairs' were erected to house imported cattle.

The decline in canal traffic continued and a real sign of the times came in 1886 when Crawshays decided to send the output of their works by rail. On 6 December 1898 mining subsidence forced the closure of the canal between Abercynon and Merthyr. The Marquess of Bute had gained control of the Glamorganshire Canal Company by 1885 and proposed converting the whole canal into a railway, an idea which was rejected by Parliament. Other stretches of the canal would be shut down over the next fifteen years, although a few boats continued to operate between Cardiff and Pontypridd until 1942.

Penarth Dock

The first part of the Bute East Dock opened in July 1855 and five months later – on 21 December – the Taff Vale Railway brought in the first trainload of steam coal from the Rhondda valleys. The new Rhymney Railway was connected to the dock in 1857, opening up another important catchment area – the Monmouthshire valleys – at the expense of Newport. The Rhymney Railway was favoured by the Bute trustees because the Managing Trustee, John Boyle, was also chairman of the board of directors of the Rhymney Railway. He did all that he could to further the interests of his own railway, which was given the largest allocation of quay space at the new dock, and was allowed free use of the coal tips. The TVR on the other hand could use only three tips, which had to be approached over the Rhymney Railway's track, a privilege for which the TVR had to pay. By 1859 Boyle's railway company controlled eleven of the seventeen tips at the East Dock as well as the seven at the Tidal Harbour.

The Taff Vale Railway's response to the Bute managers was to revive the idea of building a competing dock, free from Bute control. The *Ely Tidal Harbour* Bill and the *Penarth Harbour, Dock and Railway* Act (1857) authorised the TVR to lease, for 999 years, the new dock, basin, tidal harbour and railway. Ely Tidal Harbour, on the north bank of the Ely estuary, equipped with twelve coal tips and three steam ballast cranes, opened on 4 July 1859. The new Penarth Dock of 1865 measured 640m x 113m. There were twelve coal staithes: eight single which could load 150 tons an hour, and two which worked at twice that rate. The opening ceremony was on 10 June 1865 when, according to the *Cardiff Times*, 'The streets of Cardiff resounded with the notes of the bugle, summoning the artillery volunteers, by whom four guns, and two ammunition wagons of the First Glamorganshire Brigade were conveyed to Penarth, and placed in position on the hill overlooking the dock.' Crowds of people occupied every vantage point to watch the first vessel to enter, which was the *William Cory*, dressed overall with flags, and described as 'the largest collier afloat, carrying 1650 tons of cargo'.

Rowing in the procession of boats came the Penarth lifeboat, which was named (according to the *Cardiff Times*) 'by throwing a bottle of wine at it... The lifeboat crew then went through their evolutions in the basin, upsetting the boat, righting her, swimming and diving about in the water.' Their six-oared boat had arrived by rail in January 1861, to be housed in a newly built structure to the west of Penarth Head. (A new boat was provided in 1875 and a new lifeboat-house opened nine years later, near the entrance to the dock. There were to be two further lifeboats, before the station closed in 1905.)

After the formal opening of the dock there was breakfast for 350 followed by speeches and toasts. Singled out for particular praise by the vice-chairman of the Penarth Dock

24 Penarth Dock in the year of its opening, 1865.

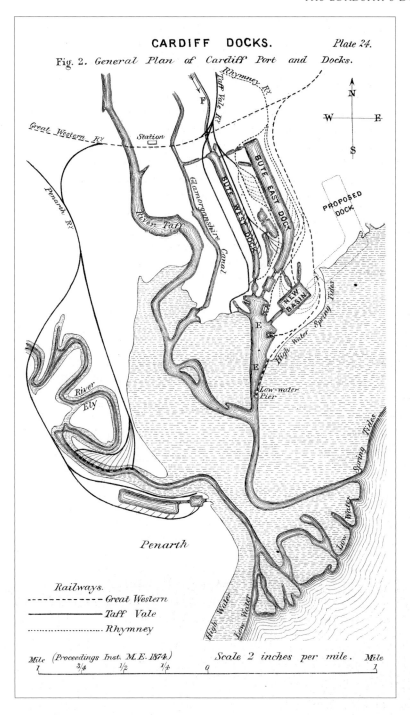

CARDIFF DOCKS. *Plate 24.*

Fig. 2. General Plan of Cardiff Port and Docks.

25 Plan of Cardiff and Penarth Docks in 1874.

Company was shipbuilder John Batchelor who 'had never been absent from any meeting, or neglected the slightest opportunity of promoting the interests of the company'. A couple of days later the *William Cory*, fully loaded and going too fast, managed to collide with the dock gates, causing them some damage. The local newspaper took up the story: 'As if this was not enough ill-luck for once, a seaman from the *William Cory* fell into the basin shortly after, being drunk, and after being rescued, seeing his cap in the water, was insane enough to jump in again after it, but was again got out safely.'

When the dock opened, the population of Penarth stood at only 1,400, but soon more people came to live and work there. By 1871 a local directory would be able to list a growing number of trades depending on maritime activities, including ship-smiths, engineers, shipwrights, boat builders, a marine store dealer, channel pilots and master mariners. For Penarth Dock there was 'The *Kate* steamer, from Bute Docks, Cardiff, running every half hour, to and fro, during tide time' and the 'Penarth Ferry – A steamboat plies across the Tidal Harbour, running day and night'. From June 1865 a chain ferry, worked by a windlass, began a service across the River Ely from Ferry Road to Penarth.

Within five years 1,250,000 tons of coal a year were being exported through Penarth Dock. The new extension brought into use in 1884 added 113m (and four more coal tips) to the dock, and by 1895 the yearly export tonnage of coal had reached 2.5 millions.

A further response to the problems at the Bute Docks was the opening of Barry Dock in 1889, with good rail links to the collieries. In its first full year of operation, 3.2 million tons of coal went out through Barry. Twelve years later Barry was exporting more coal than Cardiff, dealing with over 11,000,000 tons in the last year before the First World War.

5

SHIPS, OWNERS AND BUILDERS

The anchorage of Penarth Roads extends from Lavernock Point to the Cardiff Grounds, which are ridges of hard sand stretching across Cardiff Bay. Around the middle of the nineteenth century the Roads were generally packed with vessels, waiting for a berth or for a change of tide or wind. The *Cardiff Times* of 26 February 1859 reported, 'A Magnificent Spectacle. The immense fleet of ships, numbering nearly 800 sail, which have been accumulating for weeks past, took their departure from Penarth Roads on the favourable change of wind which took place in the beginning of the week.'

The *Bristol Channel Pilot* warned in the same year that, 'The space between Flat Holm and Lavernock Point is much frequented, not only by numerous coasters and other vessels proceeding to Cardiff, but by the Bristol and Newport traders and the steam packets, who creep up the north shore against the ebb'.

In the mid-1860s, 65 per cent of vessel departures from Cardiff were in the coastwise trade, and 90 per cent of the coal loaded at the port was carried by sailing vessels. The Severn Sea as a whole swarmed with vessels under sail. There were, according to Clayton's 1865 *Register of Shipping* (which was compiled from Customs records), sixty-eight sailing vessels registered at Cardiff, with about eighty owned at Swansea, over 100 each at Newport and Bideford and 265 at Bristol. The traditional method of financing ownership of such vessels was by division into sixty-four shares, with one person designated as 'managing owner'. Fifty people were listed at Cardiff as managing owners in 1865, some managing several, but the majority – 80 per cent – operated a single vessel. The Cardiff sailing vessels listed in Clayton's *Register* consisted (apart from small coastal traders such as sloops) of nineteen schooners, fifteen brigs, fifteen barques, seven brigantines and five ship-rigged vessels. A number of these were employed in the timber trade – 103,170 loads were imported in 1865 – often voyaging to the east coast of North America. Wooden ships could be built there (in places such as New Brunswick, Nova Scotia, Prince Edward Island and Quebec) at lower cost and in less time than in Britain, and it was often worthwhile for a timber merchant to buy a newly-built vessel, load it with timber and sail it home. The vessel could then be sold at a profit or, of course, used for future voyages.

Some of the vesssels on the 1865 Cardiff Register were:

26 Sailing vessels which could have been seen at Cardiff and Penarth in the 1860s.
Top left: a ship. Top right: a barque. Centre left: a three-masted schooner. Centre right: a topsail schooner. Bottom left: a brig. Bottom right: a brigantine.

Alexandrine (133). A brig, 24m x 7m, built at Agde in the south of France in 1847. Owners: Thomas Plain and George Davies. The vessel was lost in February 1865.

Argentinus (503). A barque, 39.3m long, built at Tatamagouche, Nova Scotia in 1857. Owner: Thomas Plain. Lost in May 1865 on a voyage from Cardiff to Quebec.

Charlotte Harrison (530). A barque, 36.5m by 9m, built in Quebec at the yard of Pierre Labbé in 1841. From around 1844 sailed from Liverpool and the Clyde to places such as Demarara, New Orleans and New York (she arrived at New York, for example, on 13 July 1850, thirty-five days out from Greenock, with a cargo of pig iron and 220 immigrants). The vessel was registered at Cardiff from 23 July 1859. Owners: Richard Verity (shipowner) thirty-two shares; William Coward (master mariner) twenty-four shares; Rees Lewis (draper) eight shares. The *Charlotte Harrison* was lost at Cape Breton Island on 17 June 1874.

Curraghmore (313). Built at Waterford in 1841, the barque was employed carrying emigrants to North America. By 1865 the vessel was owned by Thomas Elliott, but was lost in the Bristol Channel in March 1871.

Eroe (217). A brig, 26.3m in length, built at Malta in 1833. Owners: R. and J. Cory. Lost on 28 November 1873, after becoming stranded on Scroby Sands, off Great Yarmouth.

Huron (428). Built in 1841 by William Cummings at St Patrick, Charlotte County, New Brunswick. A barque, 35m long, the managing owners at Cardiff were Thomas Plain and George Davies, who held thirty-two shares between them. Sixteen shares each were held by William Coward 'robe maker' and Richard Verity 'ship's chandler'. The vessel was sold to foreign owners in September 1873.

John Henry (512). A barque, built at Newport, Monmouthshire, in 1850. Owned in 1865 by John Cory and sold to Constantinople in 1881, for use as a hulk.

Marquis of Bute (562). A barque, built in 1840. Owner: William Alexander. The vessel was noticed by the *Quebec Morning Chronicle* in May 1847: 'Chinese Produce. The vessel *Marquis of Bute*, arrived from Canton, has brought in addition to nearly 9000 packages of tea, 51 rolls of Chinese matting, 40 cases of paper, 30 cases of china-ware, several of ivory ware, 40 boxes of quicksilver, 34 of nankeens, 60 of silks, the large number of 20,000 partridge canes, and a variety of other merchandise, the production of the Chinese empire, being one of the most varied cargoes from that country which has come under our observation'.

Monnequash (522). Built at St John's, New Brunwick, in 1856. The barque was 45m long, owned by Richard Verity and Thomas Plain. Voyages between 1864 and 1866 were: Alexandria – Cardiff; Cardiff – Cape Verde; St Vincent – Quebec; Quebec – Cardiff; Cardiff – Trieste; Trieste – Liverpool; Cardiff – Alexandria; Alexandria – Cardiff. Wrecked off Prince Edward Island in October 1867.

Porto Novo (349). A barque, built in London in 1848. Owned by William Alexander, lost in the St Lawrence in September 1864.

Richard Tredwen (123). A wooden brigantine, built in 1857, owned originally by Richard Benbough (master mariner of Solva, Pembrokeshire) and Thomas Hodge (shipbuilder of Cardiff). From 1862 Thomas Hodge was sole owner.

There were only three steam vessels registered at Cardiff in 1865, although steamboats were proliferating in other ports: there were sixteen at Bristol, thirty-one at Sunderland, sixty-five at Hull and 143 at Glasgow, as well as even larger numbers at Liverpool and London. Clayton's *Register of Shipping* lists the steamers belonging to Cardiff as *Swift* (23), built in 1841, managing owner J.H. Insole; *Taff* (25) 1841, James Ware; and *Velindra* (73) 1860, which belonged to the Cardiff Steam Navigation Company. Other early small steam paddlers (all about 26m long and 5m broad) owned at Cardiff were: *Star* (15), rigged as a sloop. It was owned by Joseph Hazell, who sold it to Nantes in November 1865; *United States* (98), built at South Shields and owned by the Bute Dock Towing Company; *Pleiades* (78), built at Walker, on the Tyne, in 1858. Registered at Cardiff on 28 August 1866 by the owners Richard Morgan (master mariner) and John Brown (engineer); *Tubal Cain* (57), built at North Shields in 1860. The owner was Nicholas Strong, until the craft was broken up at Gloucester in 1889; *Black Eagle* (65) was built in 1861 on the Tyne. The vessel was owned by Nicholas Strong (steamboat owner) thirty-four shares, William Strong (waterman) twenty-two shares, and Robert Hedley Strong (engineer) eight shares. The boiler of this tug exploded in November 1866, killing all those on board.

   A decade after Clayton's list, there were still about sixty wooden sailing vessels at Cardiff, but there were now fifty-two iron steamships. Ship-owners had begun to realise the need for bigger vessels, to take advantage of the export trade in coal and the opportunities for homeward loads of iron ore or pitwood. Some of the pioneers of steamship owning at Cardiff were:

Vellacott. The screw steamer *Llandaff* (280) was built at Wallsend in 1865. The hull was clinker-built with an iron frame and the vessel was rigged as a three-masted schooner, 46.5m x 7.4m. Registered at Cardiff on 12 July 1865, the owners – all of Cardiff – were: Alexander Dalziel (ten shares), William George Noble (ten shares), Charles Ellah Stalleybrass (eleven shares), John Fry (eleven shares), Henry Vellacott (eleven shares) and John Heron Wilson (eleven shares). By March 1869 the distribution of shares was listed as John Henry Vellacott (thirteen), John Fry (nine), Henry Vellacott (twelve), Alexander Dalziel, merchant (ten), Charles Ellah Stalleybrass, merchant (ten) and John Pybus Ingledew, solicitor (ten). *Fairwater* (384) was also built at Wallsend in 1865 – a screw steamer, schooner-rigged, with a length of 45m. Registered at Cardiff on 29 January 1866 by the owners: Henry Vellacott (twelve shares), John Heron Wilson (eleven), Charles E. Stalleybrass (eleven), J.P. Ingledew (ten), Benjamin Jenkins (ten) and Alexander Dalziel (ten).

C.E. Stalleybrass. Charles Stalleybrass, from Newcastle-upon-Tyne, part-owner of the *Llandaff* and the *Fairwater*, later acquired *Galatz* (571), *Hero* (373) and *Lisvane* (420). *Lavernock* (444) was built at Wallsend in 1874 and owned jointly with the shipbuilder

27 Steam, sail and oars at the entrance to the first Bute Dock in about 1850.

Charles Albert Schlesinger. The vessel was wrecked near Bilbao in 1878. *Llanishen* (676) – another Wallsend vessel, built in 1875 – was lost on rocks off the Lipari Islands, near Sicily, in May 1885.

The South Wales Atlantic Steamship Company, The *Western Mail* of 8 February 1872 carried an advertisement for the Great Western Steamship Line's *Arragon*, which was to leave Bristol on Wednesday 13 March, bound for New York. 'Steerage passage to New York, Baltimore, Boston, Portland or Philadelphia' would cost six guineas. The *Arragon* was to be followed at a later date by 'the fine New Screw steam-ship *Great Western*'. A week later an advertisement appeared for a rival company: 'The South Wales Atlantic Steamship Company's New, first-class, full-powered Clyde built Steamships *Glamorgan* (2,500 tons. 500hp), *Pembroke* (2,500 tons. 500HP), *Carmarthen* (3,000 tons. 600HP) or other First-class Steamers, will sail regularly between Cardiff and New York, commencing about the end of April'. The vessels had been 'built expressly for the Trade, and fitted-up with all the latest improvements for the comfort and convenience of Cabin and Steerage passengers'. The iron steamship *Glamorgan*, built by William Simons & Co. of Renfrew, made her maiden voyage in October 1872, with the identical *Pembroke* coming into service later. The steamers were not charged for their use of the Bute Docks, and their bunkers were filled with free coal, but the company was not successful. On her

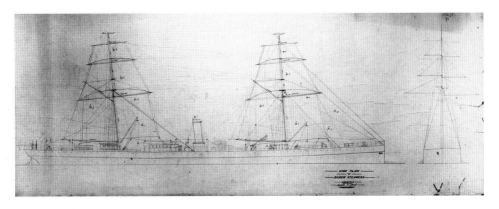

28 The *Glamorgan* of the South Wales Atlantic Steamship Company. Their *Pembroke* was an identical vessel. *Glamorgan's* maiden voyage was in October 1872, inaugurating a passenger liner service from Cardiff to New York, a venture which quickly proved to be unprofitable. *Pembroke* sank in 1881, but was salvaged. *Glamorgan* was lost in the Atlantic in March 1883.

maiden voyage the *Glamorgan* carried only thirty-nine passengers, although there was accommodation for sixty first class, sixty second class, and 480 steerage passengers. In 1873 the ship made five trips to New York, carrying a total of only 562 passengers (125 cabin and 437 steerage). The trustees wanted to cease trading in 1875 – there had been, originally, twenty trustees, but by the time of the hearing to seek a winding-up order there were only seven: the Marquess of Bute, Sir William Armstrong, C.R.M. Talbot, Colonel Crichton-Stuart, John Gilliat (a director of the Bank of England) and two directors of the Dowlais Iron Company. The hearing decided that, as the company had not been registered as a joint-stock company, the trustees were liable for the deficit of £98,000 and for the two steamships, both of which were heavily mortgaged. The registry of *Glamorgan* and *Pembroke* was transferred to Liverpool in July 1876.

Pembroke sank in 1881 after colliding with the *Ganos* of Boston; salvaged two years later, she was sold to a Spanish company and renamed *Murciano*. The first news of the loss of the *Glamorgan* – on charter to the Warren Line – came in the *Cardiff Times* of Saturday 3 March 1883: 'New York, Sunday – The White Star liner *Republic* reports meeting the steamer *Glamorgan* from Liverpool to Boston, reduced to a wreck… The steamer has been abandoned at sea'. The vessel had left the Mersey on 5 February, and made her way in stormy weather until 1.20a.m. on the 14th, when she was hit by an enormous wave, which swept overboard the captain, second officer, two seamen, a steward and two stowaways. 'The foremast, all the ventilators, the fore and main winches and pipes, the captain's room, the bridges, the steward's room, the storeroom, the passengers' rooms, all the boats, the deckhouse – everything above the deck was gone'. The steering gear was put out of action, and water poured in through the hatches, putting out the boiler fires and stopping the engines. By noon on the 16th the *Republic* had managed to pick up the forty-four survivors, losing a member of her own crew in the process.

J&M Gunn. John Gunn was born in 1837, near Thurso, making the long trek southwards at the age of eighteen to work in Newport, Monmouthshire. He moved to Cardiff in 1860. Twelve years later he was a prominent member of a group which took control of the Mount Stuart Dry Dock. In 1874, with his brother Marcus, he bought his first ship *Dunedin* (1,481) from the yard of William Doxford & Sons, Sunderland. Twenty years later the Gunns were still operating the *Dunedin*, together with *Cornelia* (894) built in 1872, *Dunbar* (1,774) built in 1876 and their newest vessel *Dunkeld* (2,791), which was fourteen years old. Their ships were all employed in the coal trade.

John Cory & Sons. John Cory was a Cornishman, seaman, and owner over the years of a few small sailing vessels. Moving to the developing port of Cardiff in 1872, he bought his first steamers two years later, from the shipbuilders Humphries of Hull: the *Ruby* (301) and the *Rothesay* (332). Within four years he was operating nine ships, adding to them by acquiring *Redbrook* (1,100), *Rhiwabon* (1,364), *Rhyl* (1,300) and *Rumney* (810) all built at Jarrow by Palmers, except *Rumney*, which was built at Sunderland by Doxfords. By 1885, with his sons Herbert and John in the business, there were seventeen vessels, and by 1889 they owned 'Cory's Buildings', a five-storey office building.

All the Cory steam vessels were acquired by setting up single-ship companies. The old way of owning by sixty-fourths was not suited to coping with the increasing cost, size and numbers of vessels, so a system of limited-liability single-ship companies came to be adopted. The cost of the ship was divided up into a large number of shares, in the hope that this would make it easier to raise the necessary finance. The shares were promoted by means of a prospectus and by newspaper advertisements, but anyone buying such shares should have been aware that it was a high-risk speculative venture, which could ruin investors if the vessel did not run at a profit. The manager of the vessel was more concerned with the earnings than the profitability of the vessel as he was, usually, paid a percentage of the gross earnings, so that as long as the ship was working – even if not making a profit – he would still be paid.

Gueret & Co. had steamships from about 1875, carrying coal to Bay of Biscay ports.

Hacquoil Brothers by 1876 owned *Brittany* (540), *Caesarea* (646) and *St Aubin* (794).

J. Marychurch owned *G.E. Wood* (698), *John Boyle* (633), *John Howard* (790), *S.W. Kelly* (675) and *W.R. Rickett* (528).

C.O. Young & Christies. Charles Octavius Young and John Robert Christie were trading with seven iron steamers in 1876: *Black Watch* (906), *Chatsworth* (620), *Free Lance* (616), *Gathorne* (772) built by Charles Hill & Sons at Cardiff, *Hellespont* (860), *Royal Welsh* (937) and *Scots Greys* (1,194).

Morel Brothers. Philip and Thomas Morel, from Jersey, came to Cardiff around 1860, setting up as ship-brokers and becoming involved in the iron ore trade, having contracts with, among others, the Aberdare Iron Company and the Dowlais Company. Their vessels, chartered as well as fully or partly owned, visited ports such as Arcachon, Bayonne, Bilbao, Brest, Caen, Cartagena and Cork.

Morel's acquired their first steamship, *Colstrup* (506) in 1876; built two years before by E.S. Swan on the Tyne, the vessel was 48m x 7.3m. Next came the *Portugalette*, built by Palmers of Jarrow and named after the port area of Bilbao. In 1882 Morels brought nine new vessels into service. By 1888 they had acquired twenty-eight vessels altogether, but lost four – *Portugalette*, which was lost in the Bristol Channel in February 1882, *Galdames* and *Collivaud* in 1886 and *Forest* in 1887. The Morel fleet was employed on what had become the typical Cardiff trading voyage, carrying coal outwards and bringing home grain and iron ore.

Turnbull Brothers. The Turnbulls were involved in shipping at Whitby where, from 1871 onwards, they built their own steamers. In 1877 the brothers Lewis and Philip Turnbull moved to Cardiff and five years later bought *Everilda* (1,455) for use on the coal and iron trades with Spain. Up to 1900 their vessels were built by the Turnbull yard at Whitby, and included *Gwendoline, Bernard, Illtyd,* and *Erie.* Their ships had all been financed on the sixty-fourth system, but the joint-stock Turnbull Brothers Shipping Company Ltd was set up in 1910.

Anning Brothers bought their first steamship *Henry Anning* in 1878, after managing sailing vessels for nearly twenty years. They traded coal to the Mediterranean, grain from the Black Sea, and iron ore from Spain. The *Henry Anning* foundered in the Bay of Biscay in 1894, bringing barley from Novorossirsk to Boston in Lincolnshire.

Evan Thomas and Henry Radcliffe. Evan Thomas (1852–91) of Aberporth was a master mariner who had learned his trade on many tramping voyages. Henry Radcliffe (1857–1921), born at Merthyr Tydfil, acquired his knowledge of the shipping business in the offices of J.H. Anning. Thomas and Radcliffe went into business together in 1881, raising the capital for a new vessel – the *Gwenllian Thomas* (1,146) – named after one of Evan Thomas's daughters. The ship's dimensions were 68m x 9.4m and it was, the partners advertised, 'most suitable for the Bilbao iron ore trade and the grain trade from the Danube, Nicolaieff and the Azoff, where she can come from her loading berth to the sea with a full cargo without the enormous expense of lighterage…'. (New railway lines were being built to connect Black Sea ports such as Nikolaiev, Novorossiisk, Odessa and Rostov with the grain-producing regions inland, encouraging the export of barley, rye and wheat). The purchase price of the *Gwenllian Thomas* was £17,750, which was raised by the traditional sixty-fourth system, with investors having to find a down-payment of one-third of the cost of their share, with the balance to be paid by instalments over two years. Of the fifty-four subscribers (some took two shares), forty-one were living in Wales. Half of all subscribers were in south Wales, with twenty from Cardiff, including such people as the Reverend J. Cynddylan Jones of Richmond Crescent; the Reverend William James of Conway Road; William Davies, grocer, of Clifton Street, Elizabeth Evans of Sapphire Street and John Jacob Davies of South Church Street. Others lived in Brixham, Hereford, Hull, London, Plymouth, Stockton-on-Tees, Malta and Sicily. *Gwenllian Thomas* arrived at Cardiff on 24 June 1882, took on her cargo of 1,457 tons of coal and set off on what would soon become a familiar voyage: coal to St Nazaire – in ballast to Bilbao – iron ore to Cardiff. *Gwenllian Thomas* was sold to a Norwegian owner in 1905 and sank, after a collision, in 1910.

Thomas and Radcliffe's second vessel, *Iolo Morgannwg* (1,882) was bought by means of a single-ship company, the Iolo Morgannwg Shipping Company. Other vessels acquired were:
1882 *Anne Thomas* (1,418). 1884 *Bala* (2,013). *Kate Thomas* (1,557). *Walter Thomas* (2,213). *Wynnstay* (1,541).

1886 *W.I. Radcliffe* (2,076).
1889 *Sarah Radcliffe* (1,440). *Mary Thomas* (2,159). *Clarissa Radcliffe* (2,544).
1890 *Douglas Hill* (2,171). *Jane Radcliffe* (1,830). *Llanberis* (2,269). *Manchester* (2,072).

Of the first fifteen vessels, ten were built at Jarrow by Palmer's Shipbuilding and Iron Company, three by Ropner & Son (established in 1888 at Stockton-on-Tees) and two by William Gray & Company at West Hartlepool.

By 1890 Thomas and Radcliffe were running sixteen single-ship companies and, as managers, taking 2.5 per cent of the gross earnings of each vessel.

Evan Thomas died in 1891, aged forty-nine, and Daniel Radcliffe joined his elder brother Henry in the firm. Daniel was twenty-four and had worked since the age of sixteen for Turnbull Brothers, and for J.H. Anning.

Evan Jones from Porthmadog, already an owner of sailing vessels at Cardiff, bought his first steamship in 1883 – the newly built *South Wales* (1,382) which was followed a year later by the *South Cambria* (2,000). His son inherited the business in 1891, and five years later was managing three steam vessels.

W. & C.T. Jones. William Jones was born at Cardiff in 1841, the son of Thomas Jones, a papermaker. William joined the army of the East India Company, rising to the rank of sergeant-major, and was at Agra and Allahabad during the Indian Mutiny. He spent some time in the United States and then in 1884, with his brothers, acquired the *Cymrodorion* (2,422). The fleet had expanded to nine by the end of the nineteenth century, all financed by the formation of single-ship companies. These were amalgamated into a new limited-liability company in 1902: 'W. & C.T. Jones Steamship Company', whose smallest vessel was *Charles T. Jones* (2,422) and the biggest *Frederick Knight* (3,599).

Jones steamers, as with all other vessels, frequently found themselves in peril. They collided or grounded in 1904 (twice), 1905 (once), 1907 (three times), 1908 (twice), 1909 (four times), 1910 (twice), 1911 (three times), 1912 (once). William Jones died in 1914, as the First World War broke out.

By the early 1880s more than 200 steamships were owned at Cardiff.

Havannah, Hamadryad *and* Thisbe

Her Majesty's Ship *Havannah*, on loan from the Royal Navy, was towed to Cardiff at the beginning of the 1860s and moored at the northern end of the East Bute Dock. Five years later the fifty-year-old sailing-vessel was to be moved to a new position on the banks of the Taff. *Havannah* was established in Cardiff as an Industrial Training Ship, several of which were put in place at various ports around Britain. They had come into being as a result of the *Industrial Schools Act* – supported by voluntary contributions, with some government finance, the hulks were provided for poor, homeless boys with the object of helping them to become merchant seamen. The 1881 census return shows seventy-nine students on board, the youngest being eight-year-old Robert Godsill of Whitchurch, Cardiff, but most boys were older – between eleven and fifteen years. Nineteen of the boys had been born in Cardiff, with a total from south Wales of about thirty. Twenty-seven came from Herefordshire or Gloucestershire, including fourteen from Cheltenham. The *Havannah* was to be a fixture at Cardiff until 1905.

Hamadryad arrived in 1866 to be fitted out as a seamen's hospital. The vessel was a Royal Navy frigate of the *Leda* class, of which nearly fifty had been built between 1800 and 1830 to a design based on the *Hebe,* a French vessel captured in 1782. *Hamadryad,* launched in 1833, was 46m long at the lower deck and 12m wide. When in service there was a crew of about 280; as a hospital it admitted up to fifty patients, financed by a levy of 2*s* per 1,000 registered tons on vessels entering the port. The *Hamadryad* was replaced by the Royal Hamadryad Seamen's Hospital, a new building officially opened by the 4th Marquess of Bute on 29 June 1905.

HMS *Thisbe* was another frigate of the *Leda* class, launched in 1824, loaned in 1863 to the Missions to Seamen and based in the West Dock until 1892. The chaplain's *Annual Report* for 1885 records his mission's activities, reporting that 2,470 visits had been made to ships, 1,552 to boarding houses, 257 to sailors' homes and 123 to the hospital ship. In his work the chaplain had forty-nine 'helpers' and thirty 'associates'. Attendance at the weekly religious services totalled 10,164 in the year. The report describes the conditions faced by merchant seaman at that time: 'Owing to the depressed state of trade our poor seamen in many cases are suffering great privation, some of them are penniless, homeless and well-nigh friendless men, not tasting food for days together.' The Mission supplied 'a good supper of bread, meat and coffee'.

The Missions to Seamen also maintained a Seamen's Church and Institute near the entrance to Penarth Dock. The *Annual Report* for 1898 stressed its usefulness:

> The postmen on their daily rounds left sailors' letters; later on sailors dropped in to find and answer them. Others came to see *The Shipping Gazette,* to make inquiries about 'berths,' 'lodgings,' 'the arrival of expected vessels,' or about 'the movement of vessels in the dock'. Some wanted a cup of coffee, a rest and a read, or it might be a quiet game of draughts, ninepins, bagatelle, or dominoes. Some had bags of clothes to leave, others bags to take away, while some, wanting to be spared a climb up the stiff hill, at the foot of which lies the dock, turned in for dinner, later on for tea, and later still for a strum on the ever popular piano.

Another religious organisation active at Cardiff Docks was the Lutheran 'Norwegian Seamen's Mission', which was founded in 1864, posting its first chaplains to Leith, Newcastle and Antwerp in 1865, and to Cardiff in 1866. Two years later a church and reading room for Norwegian sailors was built between the East and West Docks. Over the years the numbers in the congregation dwindled and the church closed in 1974, to be dismantled in 1987 and reconstructed on its new site in 1991–92.

Havannah, Hamadryad and Thisbe were all redundant sailing ships, but it should not be thought that sail was disappearing altogether. For long-distance, ocean-going voyages there were increasing numbers of steamers, but sailing vessels continued to be used for some bulk cargoes. As far as the coastal trade is concerned, more and more steam coasters appeared in the 1890s, but there were still hundreds of small wooden sailing vessels in use, known by names such as trows, sloops, ketches, and schooners. There was still a busy trade with Bristol, but also with Bridgwater where the dock, opened in 1841, sent out cargoes of bricks and handled return cargoes of coal from the Forest of Dean and south Wales. By 1874 there were over 100 vessels registered at Bridgwater, one third of them being trows. Watchet was another busy harbour, and in the middle years of the nineteenth century around 5,000 tons of iron ore were being shipped across to Wales annually, with coal being carried on the homeward voyage.

29 *Industry*, a Severn trow built in 1871, rigged as a smack. Very small vessels like this provided important links between harbours around the Severn Sea.

A good deal of the local trade – often coal and ore – was carried by Severn trows. In the 1860s Samuel Danks owned ten iron trows (of about 40 tons each) four of which had been built in Cardiff, perhaps by the Batchelors. Danks, Venn and Company – their Cardiff agent was Alfred Barfoot, based at West Bute Dock – grew to be the largest carriers on the Bristol Channel, and later became the 'Severn and Canal Carrying and Steam Towing Company'.

Sailing vessels were still used by the Bristol Channel pilots. These craft cruised down the Channel looking for a ship in need of a pilot, but this practice was abandoned in 1913 when the pilots agreed to a more co-operative scheme, using steam cutters working from fixed pilot stations at Nash Point, Barry Roads and Cardiff Roads.

There were major developments in the design of steamers coming into service. There were some tankers which carried oil from the United States and the Black Sea to Europe, but most vessels entering the Bute Docks were dry cargo carriers, for coal, grain and timber. By the early 1850s the screw steamer, as opposed to the paddler, was in common use, and most British cargoes to the Mediterranean were carried by iron screw-driven vessels. During the 1850s and 1860s steamship operation became more cost-effective as the development of the compound engine cut coal consumption by almost half. This was followed by the triple-expansion engine (and, in 1884, the invention of the marine turbine by Charles Parsons) and the development of boilers which could take higher temperatures.

A modern cargo vessel of this period could achieve 8 knots or so in good weather and was likely to carry sails, which could be used to cut down on coal consumption or if the engines broke down. There were three holds, into which cargo was loaded through three hatchways by means of steam-powered winches.

The crew might number about two dozen, including six firemen and eight seamen who lived in the forecastle, which was usually damp and subjected to every movement of the ship. The accommodation was basic and the food often inadequate.

There was increasing concern about the state in which many ships were sent to sea, and in 1836 a Select Committee of the House of Commons inquired into the causes of the considerable number of shipwrecks, finding that many vessels were badly designed, not properly built and poorly equipped. They were often not maintained properly, and frequently overloaded. Masters and mates were not always competent, or sober. The Select Committee asked consuls to report on the competence of the masters of British ships. From Odessa: 'Some ship's masters are painfully illiterate.' Our man in Pernambuco reported that most British ships were shorthanded, and the crews complained of brutality and starvation. From Danzig: 'Taken as a whole, there is not – and I say it with regret – a more troublesome and thoughtless set of men… to be met with than British merchant seamen'.

The *Merchant Shipping Acts* (1850 and 1854) brought in compulsory examinations for masters and mates.

Some Local Marine Casualties

1859 At 10.30a.m. on Tuesday 22 February 1859 the boiler of the tug *Black Eagle* exploded, killing eight people and seriously injuring others. The vessel had been bought second-hand in London by Thomas Elliott, and had left the Thames on Friday18th, arriving at the Bute Docks on the morning of Tuesday 22nd. The *Black Eagle* was towing the Sunderland brig *Milo* out of the dock when the explosion hurled debris over a wide area – a heavy chunk of iron crashed through a roof 150 yards away. The cause of the tragedy seems to have been that there was not enough water in the boiler.

The Dartmouth schooner *Amilia* was lost in a gale off Penarth. The four men on board were saved. The schooner *Kingston* of Cork was wrecked at Penarth head, but the crew of six survived.

1863 The ship *Jupiter* of London collided with the barque *Ellings,* but no lives were lost.

1864 The *Far West* got into difficulties at night, near the end of a voyage carrying guano from Calleo to Newport. The Penarth lifeboat was towed to the scene by a paddle tug, and the lifeboat's crew helped to bring the vessel under control, before she was taken to Bristol by the tugs *Iron Duke, Marquis* and *Pilot.*

1866 The barque *Jacques* of St Malo collided with *Industrie* of Hamburg. *Claudia,* a brig from Belfast, got on to a sandbank in the dark, and the Penarth lifeboat men helped to move the vessel to safety. The barque *Bonanza* of Dundee was wrecked on Barry Island, with only three survivors.

On 1 November 1866 the Cardiff tugboat *Black Eagle No. 2* was towing the Norwegian barque *Aucutor* down the Avon from the Cumberland Basin, Bristol. At about 1.45p.m. the boiler exploded, killing all on board and damaging nearby houses. The captain was William Woodman, of 9 South William Street, Cardiff, who had commanded the tug for about three years. Mate James Livings was of the same address. The engineer, George Ledger, lived at 27 South William Street. It was thought that there were perhaps four other people on board. *Black Eagle*, owned by Nicholas Strong and his two sons, was a wooden vessel built in 1861. New boilers had been fitted in September 1863. Nicholas Strong stated at the inquest that the boilers should be able to take pressures of 40 pounds per square inch, but the usual operating level was 18 psi. Two expert engineer witnesses came to the conclusion that the boiler exploded because there was not enough water in it.

1869 The steamship *Golden Fleece* sank near Barry.

1870 The Cardiff pilot cutter *Dasher* hit the Tusker Rock in thick fog. Three men were rescued by the Porthcawl lifeboat.

1872 Penarth lifeboat went to help the barque *Eleanor*, which was stuck on a sandbank, taking off most of the crew. The lifeboatmen had rowed off from Penarth at 10.00p.m. and returned at 2.30 the following morning. While this was going on the *Mystery* was in danger – this small craft was used to service the local military installations and had left Flat Holm for Brean Down, near Weston, carrying twelve soldiers and a crew of two. The gale forced them to seek refuge in Penarth Roads, where *Mystery* was dismasted after colliding with the schooner *John Pearce* of Fowey. All those on board were rescued by the men on the schooner.

1880 The sloop *Unity* of Appledore sank off Sully Island after colliding with the tug *Earl of Windsor*. The crew of two were saved by the tug.

1881 A storm forced twenty vessels on to the Penarth shores, among them *Etta* of Liverpool, *Buckingham* and *Mirella*, both of London – all three were full-rigged ships. The *County of Haddington*, which had left Penarth with a cargo of coal, had to return for repairs.

1886 On Monday 8 March six men died at the Bute Docks when the boiler of the tug *Rifleman* exploded. William Hunt was on board the Italian barque *Clotilde* and was killed after being hit by parts of the boiler. The inquest jury's verdict was that the explosion had been caused by 'over-pressure of steam, which was caused by a pin or stud that was in the cover of the governing valve, this being screwed down to prevent the escape of steam; and we also believe that the lower valve was over-loaded'.

Malleny sailed from Cardiff for Rio de Janeiro with a cargo of coal, and was towed by a tugboat as far as Lundy. After the tug left the weather got worse, so *Malleny* made for the shelter of Swansea Bay. With no steering following the loss of her rudder, the ship hit the Tusker Rock. *Malleny* finally went aground on the coast of north Devon. All twenty of the crew were lost.

Teviotdale (1,695) left Cardiff for Bombay, with a cargo of coal. Built on the Clyde in 1882, the *Teviotdale* was a four-masted iron barque which ended up on Cefn Sidan Sands, with the loss of sixteen men.

1891 The steamer *Cleveland* ran aground in fog near Lavernock Point and became a total loss, but the crew were saved. The trow *Bristol Packet* of Gloucester foundered with all hands. *Drumblair* became stuck on Sully Island and the crew had to be rescued by lifeboat.

1893 The steamship *Camargo* of Newport sank off Sully after a collision with the *Biscaye*. All were saved.

1894 Two steam vessels – the *Clytha* of Newport and the *Cadoxton* of Cardiff – collided off Barry. Seven of the *Clytha*'s crew drowned.

Henry, a sloop of Minehead, sank near Barry. Four people were rescued by the cutter *Reindeer*.

1899 The Morel steamer *Aberdare* and the *Nioba* of Glasgow collided off Sully. *Aberdare* was a total loss, but seventeen of the crew were saved.

Shipbuilding

Many small wooden boats were built by local craftsmen – no 'yard' was needed because a boat could be built on any piece of ground next to a river or harbour. As demand grew for larger vessels, and particularly after they began to be made of iron, specialist building and repairing yards came into being. Shipbuilders at Cardiff included Richard Tredwen (St Mary Street), William Davies (at the canal wharf), Thomas Jenkin, Richard Henry Mitchell, Joseph Davies, William Jones, Batchelor Brothers, Charles Hill, Norman Scott Russell, Maudsley's, J&M Gunn, Elliott & Jeffrey, and Parfitt & Jenkins. For most, the 'bread and butter' work was the repair and maintenance of existing vessels, the building of small craft, and the occasional larger one.

Batchelor Brothers

John Batchelor, born in 1820, learned his trade with shipbuilders in Sunderland, Scotland and New Brunswick. In 1843 he and his younger brother, James Sydney Batchelor, bought the yard of William Jones in Cardiff and developed timber yards locally, in Aberdare and in Merthyr. John Batchelor was active in local politics as a Liberal, and generally opposed the policies of the Bute faction. He became well known for his

30 Boat-building in *c.* 1860.

opposition to the Corn Laws, campaigned for proper sanitation and drainage for Cardiff, and was later an active promoter of the new Penarth Dock. In 1843 he was elected to the Board of Guardians, and became Mayor in 1853 at the age of thirty-three.

The Batchelors' yard was on the Taff, near St Mary Street. The *Cardiff and Merthyr Guardian* reported the launching of a boat, after sunset, on Saturday 10 March 1849. On Sunday morning the vessel was found to be stuck, and a channel had to be dredged to free it. This was probably the last launch from that yard, because of the planned diversion of the river, and the brothers moved to a new site near the entrance to the Bute Dock. They acted as ship-brokers, owned some vessels, ran a busy repair business, and built vessels to order or as a speculation.

Batchelor Brothers went bankrupt in 1872, a state of affairs brought about, some suggested, through the influence of John Batchelor's political opponents, the marquess's men. He was appointed 'Inspector of Coal' by the Crown Agents (which involved examining the quality of coal which the government was sending to the colonies), became chairman of the School Boards of both Cardiff and Penarth and, from 1877, was a partner in a china clay operation in Cornwall. He died on 30 May 1883. His statue stands in The Hayes, sculpted in 1885 by James Milo ap Griffith, and bearing the inscription 'The Friend of Freedom'.

Some of the vessels built or owned by the Batchelors were:

31 John Batchelor, Cardiff shipbuilder and 'The Friend of Freedom'.

Ely. A two-masted brigantine, 22.5m x 5m, afterwards operated in partnership with brother Thomas Benjamin Batchelor. In 1849 they had a £400 share in the *Ely* and interests in the barques *Radiant* (built at Sunderland in 1844 and sold to Liverpool owners in 1853) and *Eldon*, which was built in Quebec in 1848. Running aground in November of that year, she was salvaged, rebuilt by Batchelor Brothers, and sold in 1852. The buyers were Henry Gillespie of Cardigan, Bethel Williams of Aberdare, James Penwarden Snell of London, Thomas Holman of Topsham and J. and R. Cory of Cardiff.

Rhondda. A 28m long barque

1851 *Taff.* A barque. Launched in May, and intended for carrying emigrants, the maiden voyage in June was to New York.

1852 *Henry Gillespie.* A barque, sold to Whitehaven.

1854 *Ogmore.*

Batchelor Brothers repaired forty-eight vessels in 1855; sixty in 1856 and seventy-one in 1857.

1857 *Gabalfa* (419). A barque built for Joseph Steele of London. The Batchelors owned the barque *Harriet Sophia*, built at Pugwash, Nova Scotia.

1859 *Empress of India* (766). A full-rigged ship. Forty-three shares were bought by William Nichol of Liverpool on 9 April 1859, the Batchelors retaining twenty-one shares.

1861 *Rosario.* Broken up in 1891, when it was owned in Mauritius, and *Gabalfa.*

1863 *St Fillians.* 52m x 10.6m, built with iron beams, and *Cornelius.*

1865 *Navigator.* A brigantine, re-rigged in 1895 as a schooner. Lost at Kingston Dock, Glasgow, on 18 June 1914. The vessel had just brought a cargo of china clay from Teignmouth to Glasgow when a warehouse caught fire, destroying *Navigator* and other vessels.

1866 *Saint Vincent.* An iron paddle steamer, which was still working in 1900.

1867 *Italy.* Wrecked in 1886.

1870 *Glamorganshire.* A wooden sailing ship, and *Lion.*

On 15 April 1871, 130 of Batchelors' workers went on strike, asking for an extra shilling a week.

1871 *Hercules.* A steam paddle tugboat and *E.S. Judkins* a collier.

1872 *Ella Nicholl.* A wooden sailing vessel for Edward Nicholl of Cardiff.

James Marychurch (574). An iron screw steamer, owned by J.G. Marychurch. The vessel left Sydney, Cape Breton, on 27 October 1872, and was not heard of again.

Charles Hill & Sons Ltd

1857 Hill's of Bristol established dry docks at Cardiff. As well as repairing ships they built five vessels:

1862 *Hind* (127). A wooden schooner.

1865 *Delta* (567). An iron barque. *The Cambrian* newspaper of 30 June 1865 gives an account of the launch of the *Delta*, which was 55m long, 9m broad and with a depth of hold of 5m. This vessel, built for H. Bath & Co. of Swansea, was reported to be the first iron sailing vessel to be constructed at Cardiff – the iron was from Dowlais – and was launched sideways to the cheering of thousands, the firing of cannon, and 'Rule Britannia' played by the band of the Artillery Volunteers. The ship's builders gave a 'champagne luncheon' for 300, which began at 1.00p.m. and ended four hours later – after over twenty toasts and speeches. In replying to the toast 'The Bishop and clergy' Canon Morgan of St Mary's hoped that the launch 'was but the commencement of a trade which would afford a large amount of employment to the Messrs. Hill, Russell, Batchelor and Hodge, and they would soon rival other shipbuilding towns on the Clyde, the Thames, and other large rivers'. This hope was never fulfilled, but Cardiff did become an important ship repair centre.

In the same year the wooden sailing ship *Commander-in-Chief* caught fire in the dry dock, and burned to the ground. The vessel had loaded half of her cargo of patent fuel, which may well have been the seat of the blaze.

After *Delta* Hill's built:

1869 *Rookwood* (770). An iron barque, which cost £11,000, and was operated by Hill's until 1896.

1871 *Hector.* An iron tugboat.

1873 *Gathorne* (772). An iron steamship, with an auxiliary schooner rig. Owned by Charles Octavius Young and John Robert Christie; sold to Spain in 1878.

Norman Scott Russell

Norman Scott Russell's yard built the *Mallorca* in 1864. This vessel, an iron paddle steamship (71m x 7.9m and capable of 12 knots), was launched in November 1864 for the Empresa Mallorquina de Vapores (Majorcan Steamship Company). The *Cardiff Times* of 18 November reported that, 'On Wednesday morning, from an early hour, crowds of pedestrians and numbers of carriages might have been seen wending their way towards the mouth of the river Taff' and to the new ship-building yard of Mr N. Scott Russell. The newspaper described the new vessel as: 'The first iron ocean-going steamship ever built in Cardiff'. The iron was supplied by the Dowlais Company, and the 180hp oscillating engines were designed by Scott Russell & Co and built by Jackson and Watkins. 450 tons of cargo and coal could be carried, as well as passengers. The figurehead was 'a lion rampant, supporting the arms of Majorca in gold and heraldic colours, and the stern is ornamented with foliage, vine leaves and grapes, gilded'. Below the figurehead a platform had been erected from which Mrs Clark – wife of G.T. Clark of Dowlais – named the *Mallorca* by smashing a bottle of champagne.

The newspaper's reporter went on to describe changes made in the yard since last summer: the large machine shop had been doubled in length and increased in width; a high stone wall had been built around the yard, and 'a massive pair of gates erected fronting the canal with *Bute Iron Works 1864* graven on a granite slab over the side door'. The office buildings are two storeys high, and the carpenters and moulders shops are connected with each other by a bridge. 'The long, wide, dreary expanse of mud and marsh, from the Taff to the Ely, does not look so interminable and dreary now that signs of life and animation are beginning to appear along the bank of the Taff'.

After the launch the official party retired to the upper floor of the office block, where breakfast was provided by the Angel Hotel. In one of the many speeches Norman's father, John Scott Russell (who had built the *Great Eastern* and HMS *Warrior* in his yard at Millwall) described how his son 'having seen a great deal of ship-building on the Thames and in foreign countries' had come to set up as a ship-builder in Cardiff, which had 'growth like that of an American city rather than like any town in England'.

The celebrations continued in the evening, with a dinner at the Angel. The *Mallorca* left Cardiff on 25 February 1865, arriving at Palma de Majorca on 7 March and entering service on the Palma to Barcelona route on 4 April. *Mallorca* continued in this role for twenty-five years before being broken up at Barcelona in 1892.

J&M Gunn built paddle-propelled tug boats including the iron vessels *Dunrobin* (109) in 1876 and the 'passenger-carrying tug' *Empress of India* (160), both of which were built for the Strong family.

The main business of *Parfitt and Jenkins* was making boilers and building steam-engines, and between 1869 and 1881 they built thirteen shunting locomotives for the Bute Docks. In addition they launched:

1870 *Bee* (31). A passenger tender for the Portishead Railway Company. Sold to Bristol Corporation in 1888. Became the *Gaer* of Newport in 1912.

1871 *Druid* (129). A packet steamer which was employed on the Cardiff to Bristol service.

1872 *John Boyle* (633). A steamship. The vessel was owned in the traditional sixty-fourth manner by: George Sully Stowe, a shipping and insurance broker – sixteen shares; George Parfitt, engine and shipbuilder – sixteen shares; Edward Jenkins, engine and shipbuilder – sixteen shares; William Oulton, merchant, Liverpool – sixteen shares; Thomas Sully Stowe, gentleman, Liverpool – sixteen shares; Richard Stowe, gentleman, Cardiff – sixteen shares. The vessel sank on 4 April 1876, after a collision.

1877 *Cory Brothers* (31). A screw steam vessel, with a two-masted schooner rig, built for John Cory.

Bute Shipbuilding, Engineering & Dry Dock Co.

In 1882 Morel Brothers, with half-a-dozen partners, went into business as the Bute Shipbuilding, Engineering and Dry Dock Co., taking over the existing facilities on the River Taff. The company built:

1887 *Collivaud* (950). Launched in March for Morel, replacing an earlier *Collivaud* of 1882. The maiden voyage was to Alexandria. The ship was sold in 1912.

1889 *Cardiff Castle* (1,266). Built of Dowlais steel for Morel Brothers, the vessel was launched on 26 October. The *Western Mail* reported that 'The largest ship ever built at Cardiff was successfully launched on Saturday morning from the Bute Shipbuilding, Engineering and Dry Docks Company's works, on the east bank of the River Taff.' The newspaper stated that it was the eighth ship to be launched from that yard. Designed by Thomas Dobson, *Cardiff Castle* was 'constructed on the long bridge and quarter-deck principle' and was to be fitted with triple-expansion engines of 200hp, producing a probable speed of 9 knots. After launching the vessel hit the Clarence Road Bridge, which was then being built. The maiden voyage was to Brazil. The ship was renamed *Blaenavon* in 1892 and was lost after hitting a mine in 1915.

1890 *Mayfield* (3,900). Built of Dowlais steel, with a triple-expansion engine, and launched, on 19 April 1890, for Frederick Woods of London. The maiden voyage was to Alexandria. *Mayfield* was lost in 1909, on passage from Savona to the Clyde.

Other companies set up in the 1870s and 1880s included Harvey & Son; Langmaid & Co.; Penarth Shipbuilding and Repair Co.; The Bute Shipbuilding Co. became the Mount Stuart Shipbuilding, Graving Dock & Engineering Co. Later came the Bute Dry Dock, the Cardiff Junction Dry Dock and others. At the turn of the century the Cardiff Junction Dry Dock & Engineering Company advertised that they were in business as 'Engineers, Ship Builders and Repairers, Iron and Brass Founders, Steam Engine and Boiler Makers'. They 'have every appliance in Machinery for all kinds of repairs to Steamers or Sailing Ships', and their dry dock, 'fitted complete with Electric Light,' can take steamers up to 5,000 tons.

There were two Mount Stuart Graving Docks, No.1 was 134m long and 21.3m wide; No.2 was 128m long and 32m wide and could handle two vessels side-by-side. The company announced that 'Vessels are Docked, Cleaned and Painted at Low Rates' and 'Repairs to Hull and machinery of ships executed with Despatch and Economy'.

Some small craft were built at Penarth – for example *Young Marquis* (11.9m long by 3.8 broad) constructed by George Down in 1868. At a later date the Penarth Ship Building & Ship Repairing Company advertised that they were 'Iron ship builders, engineers, boilermakers, blacksmiths, coppersmiths, Tinsmiths, Plumbers etc'. They undertook all kinds of repairs to wooden vessels and boasted of a 'Railway siding into yard'. On 7 May 1898 'amid the acclamation of more than a thousand spectators' they launched the *Eirene* (67) for the Missions to Seamen – it was a small, single-screw iron steamer, 23m long x 4.6m beam, with holds 2.6m deep.

32 The Mount Stuart Dry Docks.

The money for this new vessel had been raised by public subscription, which was started off in 1895 (according to the Mission's magazine *Word on the Waters*) with a donation of £1,000 by 'two sisters interested in sailors, and especially in lightships' crews'. The dockmasters of Barry, Cardiff and Penarth wrote to the Mission in support:

> We emphasize the fact that in 1894, 63,125 seamen were engaged, and 44,885 seamen were discharged, in our three ports alone. Of the 7,749 ships that entered and left, a large proportion were detained for some hours, at least, outside our Docks, waiting for the tide to rise sufficiently for them to enter, and were thus open to your visitation. Further, we know that, with contrary winds, fleets of over a hundred vessels are detained in our Channel, sometimes for days together and are glad of anyone to visit them.

The Missions to Seamen *Annual Report* for 1898 described the first months of the little steamer's operation:

> Services have been held in lighthouses, on the decks of light-vessels, and on the decks of fishing smacks, coasting vessels, steamers, and sailing vessels in Carmarthen Bay, Swansea Bay, and in all the roadsteads between Newport Roads and Lundy Island; scores of letters have been brought ashore and posted... Already the *Eirene* has had a sharp taste of heavy gales and dense fogs, and her skipper and his crew, five all told, an experience of anxious hours and weary long night watches... Since the *Eirene* commenced her work, and in the waters over which she travels, six pilots, one apprentice and six boatmen have been drowned; three pilot boats lost, five vessels wrecked, and one abandoned.

STEAMBOAT PASSENGER SERVICES

A Bristol to Swansea steam packet service had been inaugurated on 10 April 1823, with *Glamorgan* taking eight hours over the voyage to Swansea. For Cardiff passengers the boat stopped off Sully Island where people embarked or disembarked by clambering into or out of small boats. The Reverend Joseph Romilly described a voyage on the *Glamorgan* in his diary for 14 August 1834. He left Hotwells, Bristol, at 12.30p.m. A woman passenger had been so scared of climbing down the ladder on to the deck 'that she cried bitterly and screamed'. There were four 'cabin' passengers, who were allowed the privilege of dining with the captain. Arriving off Swansea at 10.30p.m., the *Glamorgan* anchored, and a pilot boat took some of the voyagers ashore. Passing Nash Point the *Glamorgan's* passengers might well have called to mind the wreck, just over three years before, of the Bristol-bound passenger steamer *Frolic* (108). Over fifty people lost their lives, a tragedy which led to the building of the lighthouses – a 'high' light and a 'low' light, which were about 300m apart, and intended to provide leading lights past the sandbanks.

Cardiff to Bristol

A steam packet service from Cardiff to Bristol started in 1834 with the wooden paddle vessel *Nautilus* (29m long) built by Scott's of Bristol in 1831. A journey in the after-cabin cost 6s and in the forward cabin 3s. The advent of the *Nautilus* killed off any passenger trade via Sully, and the Swansea packets began to call at Cardiff from February 1835. In July of that year the *Lady Charlotte* came into service, owned by the Cardiff and Bristol Steam Navigation Company, and in September made the run from Cardiff to Bristol in only two-and-a-half hours. Evidence given to a Select Committee of the House of Lords stated that in the first ten months of 1837 *Nautilus* and *Lady Charlotte* carried 12,264 passengers on their daily service between Cardiff and Bristol.

Paddle steamers employed on the route between Cardiff and Bristol included:

Joseph Tregelles Price, Neath Abbey Iron Works: *Nautilus* in service 1834–41; *Bristol* 1841–42; *Prince of Wales* 1842–45.

Cardiff and Bristol Steam Packet Company: *Lady Charlotte* 1835–47.
Bristol General Steam Navigation Co: *Star* 1847–52 and 1854–55; *Taff* (148) 1856–62 and 1864–65; *Ely* (189) 1876–79.
Cardiff Steam Navigation Co.: *Taliesin* (158) 1850–58; *Jenny Jones* (161) 1851–64, an iron screw steamer; *Velindra* 1860–67, which was described in the *Illustrated Times* of 22 December 1860:

> A new steam-vessel destined for the service between Bristol and Cardiff has just been completed by Messrs. J.T. Mare and Co., of Millwall, for the Cardiff Steam Navigation Company. This vessel, which is named *Velindra*, is of 285 tons burden, and 100-horse power, while its engines, being constructed on the oscillating principle, will work up to six times their nominal force. The dimensions of the vessel afford ample opportunity for both passenger accommodation and stowage, since her length is 160 feet, while the breadth of beam is 19 feet. Besides this she is provided with a raised quarter-deck, upon which is constructed a ladies' cabin, elegantly furnished and fitted. There is provision for both first and second class passengers, while every convenience is adopted for the transit of horses, as well as for ordinary cargo. Her average speed is about seventeen miles an hour.
>
> The long and tedious journey into South Wales, via Gloucester, may now be most agreeably diversified by travelling by rail to Bristol, and then crossing the Channel by the boats of the Cardiff Steam Navigation Company, which company justly anticipates a large accession of traffic from the attractive qualities of this their new vessel.

In the event it came to be so well regarded that in 1863 a Bristol pub was named after it – the Velindra Hotel, in Commercial Road.

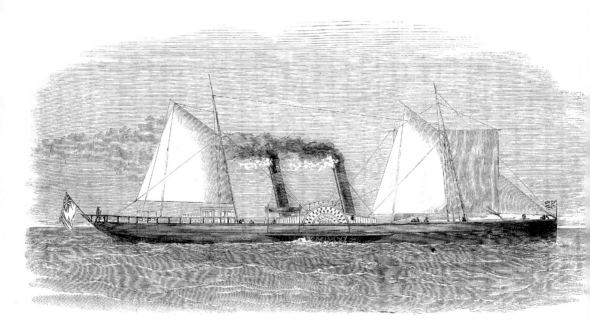

33 *Velindra*. Built at Millwall for the Cardiff Steam Navigation Company. The vessel was operated by them from 1860 to 1867, usually on the Cardiff to Bristol service.

When the Cardiff Steam Navigation Co. was wound up in 1867 *Velindra* was bought by J.W. Pockett of Swansea and employed on the Swansea to Bristol service (a voyage now of around four hours) until the route was discontinued in 1895. *Velindra* was a popular craft on her summer excursions to Ilfracombe, Padstow and Tenby, but was scrapped in 1897, after thirty-seven years of service.

Cardiff to Cork

By the middle of the century a voyage from Cardiff to Cork could be undertaken in the steamer *Osprey* at a cost of 17s 6d in 'the best cabin' and 7s as a deck passenger. 'Horses, Carriages, Live Stock and Goods intended for shipment should be alongside One Hour before the time of Sailing'. (*Cardiff Times* 5 February 1859). A steamer left Cardiff for Cork (via Milford Haven) every Wednesday and returned, direct to Cardiff, on Saturdays.

Cardiff to Portishead

In 1868 a low-water pier was opened at Cardiff, and a new pier came into use at Portishead. The Cardiff Steam Navigation Company was closed down and a new concern was set up, the Cardiff and Portishead Steamship Company, backed by the Bute Trustees. *Dart*, *Ely*, *Taff* and *Wye* were operating between 1869 and 1871, in which year the *Western Mail* advertised the *Taff* and the *Wye* as providing a daily service to and from Bathurst Basin (Bristol), calling at Portishead and Hotwells: 'After cabin 2s 6d. Fore cabin 1s 6d'. In 1871 the Bute Trustees took over *Dart* and *Wye* and acquired other vessels – all were then registered in the name of John Boyle.

John Boyle (Bute Trustees) ran services with *Dart* 1871–74, *Druid* 1871–86, *Granville* 1871–73, *Wye* 1871–74 and *The Lady Mary* 1876–86.

The functions of the Bute Trustees were transferred to the new Bute Docks Company, secretary William T. Lewis, on 1 January 1887. Their vessels were *The Lady Mary*, *Success* (94) 1887–98, and *The Marchioness* (251) 1889–1912, a steel-hulled paddle steamer.

Cardiff to Burnham-on-Sea

To try to attract traffic from boom-town Cardiff, where the second part of the Bute East Dock opened on 19 January 1858, the Somerset Central Railway Company opened a 'pier' at Burnham later in the same year, although it was really a slipway 275m long, sloping down into the water. The steamer service began on 24 May 1858 with the *Taliesin* (owned by the Cardiff Steam Navigation Company), which had been taken off its usual Cardiff to Bristol route. The vessel left Cardiff at 5.30a.m. with eighty passengers, paying 3s each, disembarking at Burnham three hours later. By 1865 the Somerset and Dorset Railway was advertising a new route from Cardiff to 'Paris, Caen, Bordeaux and the South of France (via Burnham, Poole and Cherbourg) by the Swift and Powerful steamer *Albion*'.

The Somerset Central Railway was not legally allowed to own steamers, and so a new enterprise was set up, the Burnham Tidal Harbour Company, which was based in the SCR offices at Glastonbury and with an office on Stuart Street in Cardiff. This company's vessels on the Cardiff to Burnham service were:

Ruby (174) 1860–63. An iron paddle-steamer which could make the passage in about one hour and a quarter. On 18 August 1863 she was badly damaged by going aground at Burnham pier, and was sold in the following year; *Defiance* (150) 1863–71; *Heather Bell* (152) 1864–67; *George Reed* (170) 1866–68, an iron screw steamer, which was to be wrecked off the Maldives on 17 December 1872. *Sherbro* (239) 1884–88 was originally intended for service in the colonies and named after the Sherbro people, and island, of Sierra Leone. Vessels chartered for the route included *Taliesin* 1858–60, *Pilot* 1863, *Diana* 1871, and *Flora* 1871–78.

The end of the Cardiff to Burnham ferry came with the opening of the Severn rail tunnel in 1886. The ferry service ceased in July 1888 and *Sherbro* was bought by Cantabrica Navigation Company of Bilbao.

Cardiff to Penarth

A steam service had been running from Cardiff Pier Head to Penarth from the 1850s. Penarth Dock opened in 1865, which prompted the Cardiff Steam Navigation Co. to put *Jane* and *Kate* to work – small paddle boats which provided a regular service, depending on the tide, between the Bute Docks and Penarth.

The Steam Navigation Company closed two years later, when a new partnership took over, bringing into service *La Belle Marie*. In 1883 Henry Vellacott took an interest in the firm, and it became the Cardiff and Penarth Steam Ferry Co, adding *Iona* (64) from the Penarth Shipbuilding Co. *La Belle Marie* was sold and another *Kate* (99) arrived in 1893. From May 1900 it became possible to walk from Ferry Road to Penarth using the new tunnel under the River Ely. The Cardiff to Penarth ferry ended in October 1903. (The tunnel closed on 1 October 1963.)

Excursions

The *Britannia* took people on pleasure cruises during its visit to Bristol in 1817; most of the early packet steamers ran summer excursions in addition to their timetabled services. Tugboats were often used for the same purpose, taking time off from their usual tasks of manoeuvring vessels around the docks and towing sailing ships against the prevailing winds down the Bristol Channel. Tugs owned by Strongs of Cardiff – the *Joseph Hazell*, *Advance* and *Prince Consort* – took trippers across to Weston-super-Mare or Burnham-on-Sea for many years. Their tugboat *Empress of India* was able to embark about 200 people, and was used for summer trips each year from 1878 to 1893.

The tugs *Earl of Bute*, *Earl of Jersey* (both of 146 tons, and built in 1866) and *Earl of Dunraven* (190) were chartered for excursions by Frederick Edwards and George Robertson, who had been engaged in the business since the 1840s, later trading as 'Bristol Channel Passenger Services Ltd'. Competition was intense – on 5 June 1893 *Lorna Doone* (Edwards and Robertson) collided with *Ravenswood* (P&A Campbell) as

34 *Ravenswood*. Bought by Campbell's from the builders, McNight & Co. of Ayr, in 1891. There were originally two funnels, but one was removed in 1909. The paddle steamer served as a Royal Naval vessel in two world wars.

they scrambled to be first to arrive at Weston Old Pier. The Board of Trade Inquiry decided that *Ravenswood* had been 'navigated negligently,' awarded costs of £125 against Captain Alec Campbell, and told the Weston Pier Company to employ a harbourmaster. By 1895 Edwards and Robertson had *Bonnie Doone* (built 1876), *Lorna Doone* (built 1891), *Scotia* (built 1880) and a new *Lady Margaret* (built 1895), but at the end of the year the company went out of business. The new vessel joined the Campbell fleet and the others went to John Gunn of Cardiff, who disposed of his vessels within three years, leaving the Campbells as the survivors of a lengthy struggle for supremacy.

The Campbell fleet could trace its origins to the Clyde of the 1850s, and the vessels of John, Alexander and Robert Campbell. In 1887 their *Waverley* (258) spent the summer on charter in the Bristol Channel, and Captain Alexander Campbell decided to bring the steamer back in the following year, making Bristol his base from 1889. The *Ravenswood* (391) was delivered from the builders – McKnight of Ayr – in 1891, followed by the formation of P(eter) & A(lexander) Campbell Ltd in 1893.

The Campbell fleet survived through two world wars and rode out the economic storms for many years, running scheduled services as well as pleasure cruises. Penarth had no pier until 1895 – the official opening, with the Cogan Brass Band in attendance, was on 13 April when the *Bonnie Doone* and *Waverley* embarked passengers for Weston, always a very popular destination with south Walians, but by no means the only one. Others included Ilfracombe and Minehead, and in 1906 trips were made to see HMS *Montagu*, stuck fast on the rocks of Lundy. At times of peak demand there was always a temptation to pack too many people on board: in July 1900 the master of the *Glen Rosa* was prosecuted for carrying 797 passengers when licensed for 541, and the *Scotia* was once found to be carrying 357 people over its legal maximum. The steamers were used not only for pleasure trips, but were also timetabled ferries, connecting with

35 Penarth Pier opened on 13 April 1895, when trippers for Weston-super-Mare were embarked by the paddle steamers *Bonnie Doone* and *Waverley*.

36 *Gwalia* and *Westonia*, owned by the Barry Railway Company (Red Funnel Line). *Westonia*, furthest from the camera, ended up with the rival Campbells, who gave her the name *Tintern*, and took away one funnel. She was sold to Portuguese owners in 1913, becoming the *Alentejo*. The *Gwalia* was sold in 1910, and was to be sunk in June 1940, bringing men home from the Dunkirk beaches.

rail and bus services on the other side, and convenient for people taking up employment across the water, visiting friends and relations, shopping, or delivering goods.

Competition for P&A Campbell appeared in 1905 in the form of the Barry Railway Company's *Devonia*, *Gwalia* and *Westonia*. The *Barry Railway Steam Vessels Act* of 1904 allowed the railway company to operate steamers between Barry and anywhere on the coast between Ilfracombe and Weston-super-Mare (both inclusive). It could also run summer excursions to other places, provided that the trips started and finished at Barry. The Barry Railway tried to circumvent the restrictions by putting the steamers into a holding company – the Barry and Bristol Steam Shipping Company, the 'Red Funnel Line' – and began a service from Cardiff Pier Head to Weston-super-Mare. P&A Campbell took legal action, and two years later the Barry Railway gave in, agreeing to abide by the provisions of the Act. The *Gwalia*, *Devonia* and *Westonia* were taken out of the holding company in 1908 and became directly owned by the railway company, along with the *Barry*, which had been intended for a proposed ferry service from Barry to Burnham. The fleet was sold off, and by April 1910 the four steamers were owned by Bristol Channel Passenger Boats. *Gwalia* was sold again almost immediately and the remaining three – *Barry*, *Devonia* and *Westonia* – joined Campbell's fleet in December 1911. *Westonia* was renamed *Tintern* and sold two years later to a Portuguese company as the *Alentejo*.

Over the years P&A Campbell ran some two dozen steamers, some of the earliest being: *Waverley* 1888–1920, *Ravenswood* 1891–1955, *Westward Ho* 1894–1946, *Cambria*

37 Cardiff Pier Head – arrival and departure point for P&A Campbell's 'White Funnel Fleet' of paddle steamers.

1895–1946, *Britannia* 1896–1956, *Lady Margaret* 1895–1905, *Glen Rosa* 1897–1920, *Bonnie Doone* 1899–1913, *Scotia* 1899–1903, and *Albion* 1899–1921.

38 *Britannia* joined Campbell's in 1896. One of their fastest vessels, she was recorded as having travelled from Penarth to Weston in only twenty-three minutes, and from Cardiff to Weston and back again in one hour and three minutes. *Britannia* was converted into a minesweeper in the two world wars, in the second as HMS *Skiddaw*, before being broken up at Newport in December 1956.

7

INTO THE TWENTIETH CENTURY

On 1 January 1887 Cardiff Docks were vested in a new entity, the *Bute Docks Company,* and Roath Dock was opened. Ten years later the landmark Pier Head Building was built as the Company's offices, just as the enterprise was about to change its name again, to *The Cardiff Railway Company.* The Queen Alexandra Dock (777m long and with its width varying from 244 to 305m) was opened in 1907 by King Edward VII.

Imports – mostly grain and flour, timber, and iron ore – accounted for only 20 per cent of the docks' total trade. Cardiff was the headquarters of Spillers and Bakers Ltd, flour millers, and makers of food for dogs, birds and sailors (for the latter in the shape of ships' biscuits). The company became the country's biggest importers of malting barley,

39 A three-masted schooner leaving the West Bute Dock. The Pierhead Building was built in 1896/97 as the offices of the Bute Docks Company.

grain and corn. Edward England's potato importing business was doing so well that he built his own warehouse at the docks in 1907.

The quantity of timber imported had increased from 103,170 loads in 1865 to 689,871 in 1895. According to Frank W. Hybart (Ballinger 1896), 'Cardiff now takes second place in the United Kingdom for the importation of wood goods, ranking next after London'. Cargoes arrived from Canada, the United States, Norway, and Baltic ports such as Danzig and Stettin.

A *Guide to Cardiff City and Port* told its readers that 'One of the most familiar sights at night in Cardiff is the glare in the sky caused by the blast furnace at the Dowlais Works'. The raw materials went straight from ships into railway trucks, which were then shunted off to the Works. Spanish ore arrived at the docks for the Tharsis Copper Works.

Since the 1850s the Royal Navy had preferred to use Welsh coal, and forty years later it was still favoured. At Queen Victoria's Golden Jubilee Review of the Fleet in July 1887 a *Notice to Mariners* ordered that 'All steam vessels present are required to burn the best Welsh coal, so that smoke may not obstruct the view of the Fleet nor cause danger of collision'. The demand for coal to power steamships increased eightfold between 1869 and 1913 and demand was also growing in other industries – by sevenfold for railways, while sales of coal to produce gas tripled. All this affected south Wales, as people flooded in looking for work, and by 1913 more than 60 per cent of the population of Wales was to be found in Glamorgan, where there were 323 collieries. The Rhondda collieries alone provided employment for over 41,000 people, who produced 9,611,000 tons of coal in the year.

By the 1890s Cardiff had became famous as the largest port in the world, measured by tonnage handled. Coal accounted for 97 per cent of its exports, with 70 per cent now carried by steamship. Just over a half of the coal went to Europe, and one third to South America. The boom was at its peak in 1913, when about one-third of the world's coal exports went out from south Wales.

Although there were some imports at Penarth, such as iron ore, pitwood, and pulp for making paper, the chief activity of the dock was the export of coal. In 1870 Penarth sent out just under 2 million tons, which was about 30 per cent of all the coal transported by the Taff Vale Railway. By 1912 the coal, coke and patent fuel exported through Penarth totalled 4,179,506 tons. Penarth was also equipped for ship-repair work: a slipway had been built at the tidal harbour and a floating dock came into use in April 1910.

The Workforce

The chief purpose of Cardiff and Penarth Docks was to shift coal, which arrived in trains of railway wagons, drawn by steam locomotives. In the docks the coal was handled by two groups of workers, the *tippers* and the *trimmers*. The tippers worked on the dockside, and operated the machinery that tipped the coal from the railway trucks into the ship's hold. They were employed by the docks management, and paid by the hour.

The trimmers worked on board the ship, stowing the coal so that it was evenly spread, and less likely to move during the voyage. There were three groups of trimmers – *foremen*, *gangmen*, and *hobblers*. A foreman was in charge of a number of gangs (each of half-a-dozen men) and recruited the gangmen – anyone who wanted to work was obliged to pay an 'entry fee' to the foreman. As well as this initial impost, the foreman

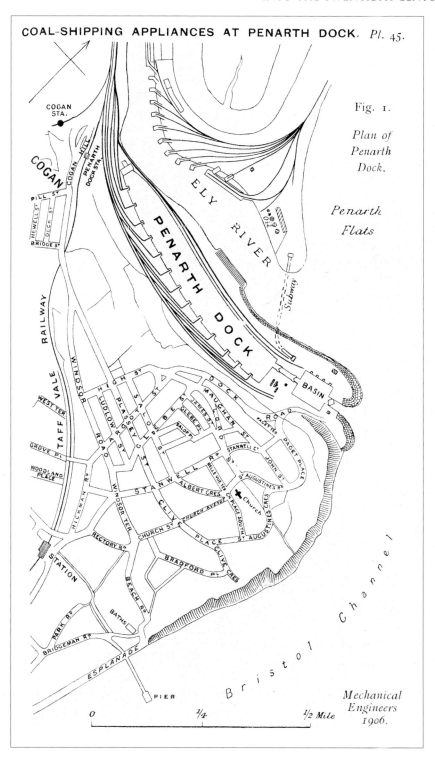

COAL-SHIPPING APPLIANCES AT PENARTH DOCK. *Pl.* 45.

Fig. 1.

*Plan of
Penarth
Dock.*

*Penarth
Flats*

*Mechanical
Engineers
1906.*

40 Plan of Penarth Dock, 1906.

41 Penarth Dock.

took a cut from the earnings of each gang. A trimming gang was paid an agreed sum for every ton of coal which had been tipped into the hold of the ship they were working on, so the fewer men in a gang, the higher each man's earnings. There were times, however, when a gang had to take on 'casual' labour to help out. These hobblers were not given a share of the tonnage payment but were paid, by the gangmen, for the number of hours worked. The hobblers, poorly paid and often with no work, wanted to be paid at the same rate as the gangmen and to have a set manning scale for trimming each vessel.

The way that trimming was organized generated conflict – between foremen and gangmen (over fees and deductions from pay, which were not abolished until 1914), and between gangmen and hobblers (there was no manning scale until 1911). The whole thing was described as 'a system of sweating and blackmailing which has no equal in this country'.

There was tension between ship-owners and shippers over which of them should control the trimming operations and, more fundamentally, whether trimming was necessary at all. There was a time when trimmers had been essential, because coal was loaded on to sailing vessels through small hatches into holds of varying size, and coal that was not properly stowed was dangerous. But now there were steamships, with easier access to the holds, and by 1887 Roath Dock had the Lewis-Hunter coaling cranes, which distributed the coal more evenly in the hold. Another innovation was the *trunk-decked* ship – from Ropner's of Stockton-on-Tees and advertised as being 'self-trimming' the first on the Cardiff register was the *Llandudno* bought by Evan Thomas Radcliffe in 1897. In spite of these technical developments, the trimmers continued to be paid for every ton of coal loaded, whether they handled it or not. The trimmers' jobs were saved by the fact that it was in a shipper's financial interest to continue the practice of trimming. The coal shipper controlled and paid the trimmers, recovering the payments (plus a management fee) from the ship's owner. The shippers negotiated the rates to be paid for trimming but, as the payment was made by somebody else, they had no incentive to keep the rates down. The owners, on the other hand, had to bear the costs of trimming, but had no control over those costs.

In 1888 the Cardiff coal trimmers formed themselves into a trade union, with just over 800 members, and by the year 1913 membership stood at over 2,000. The Cardiff Coal Trimmers' Union was not seen to be 'militant' and was characterised by Ben Tillett, the dockers' leader, as a 'benefit and sick society'.

The life of a seaman was determined, on shore as well as on the sea, by the pattern of trade. A typical tramp steamer voyage would involve carrying a bulk cargo – food or raw materials – from anywhere in the world to a European port. On board ship he had to live, usually, in the fo'c's'le, which could be squalid, crowded, and noisy, with bunks made of iron and fastened to the vibrating steel plates of the ship. He had to endure fleas and lice, coal dust, and lack of toilet facilities, as well as poor food. Most of the crew worked four hours on and four hours off – First Watch: 20.00hrs–24.00hrs; Middle Watch: 24.00hrs–04.00hrs; Morning: 04.00hrs–08.00hrs; Forenoon: 08.00hrs–12.00hrs; Afternoon: 12.00hrs–16.00hrs; then there were two shorter watches – First Dog Watch: 16.00hrs–18.00hrs; Second Dog Watch: 18.00hrs–20.00hrs. There was always something to be done to maintain the vessel – hosing coal dust off the deck, scrubbing, caulking, chipping off rust and painting. If a seaman absconded he could be charged with 'absenting himself from his ship' and sent to gaol.

At the final port of a voyage most of the crew were paid off, and would receive no more money until they signed on for another trip. To obtain a new cargo a ship could be taken to Cardiff with a skeleton crew, load another cargo of coal, and recruit a new crew. Cardiff thus became an important 'signing-on' port. In 1894, at Barry, Cardiff and Penarth, over 63,000 men signed on and nearly 45,000 were discharged. Although many seamen made their home locally, others, usually with very little money, came to look for a ship. Cardiff became known as a 'hard-up port' and its seamen's boarding-houses were 'hard-up houses'. For J. Havelock Wilson, the seamen's union leader, Cardiff was 'the most undesirable port in the United Kingdom, the dumping ground of Europe'.

Where could they stay, these men looking for work? There were a couple of sailors' homes: the Sailors' Home on Stuart Street (paid for by the Marquess of Bute) had sleeping accommodation, a library and a reading room. In the 1881 census, sixty-three boarders are listed, the youngest being sixteen-year-old John Valle, an ordinary seaman from Spain; the oldest was John Curran, able seaman, aged sixty-one, from New Brunswick. The others staying at the home came from many parts of the British Isles, and from Canada, Denmark, Germany, the Netherlands, Nova Scotia and the United States. The John Cory Sailors' and Soldiers' Rest provided a place to read, write and play some board games. For the sick there were the fifty-four beds in the Royal Hamadryad Seamen's Hospital, which in a year helped nearly 1,000 in-patients and over 3,000 out-patients.

Most men paid for a bed in one of the boarding-houses (there were nearly 200 of them) where the boarding-house keepers, known as 'boarding masters', provided the seaman not only with accommodation, but also lent him money for food and clothes. The boarding masters were a contact point for ships' masters looking to make up a crew, and provided (for a fee) quick access to a pool of out-of-work seamen. Men with no money, probably in debt to the boarding master, and anxious to get a job, could be

42 The Sailors' Home on Stuart Street, where seafarers looking for work could find temporary accommodation.

persuaded to sign on at the minimum wage rate – to the financial advantage of the ship-owner, the ship's master, and the boarding master. (The practice was known as 'crimping' – a 'crimp' was a person who made money by getting seamen to sign on to a ship.)

Up to 1881 a man signing on was given an *Advance Note* to the value of a month's pay, against which the holder could draw cash before his ship sailed. There was a tendency for a sailor and his cash to be quickly parted, and the Advance Note came to be replaced by the *Allotment Note*, by means of which the seaman could arrange for a relative (usually his wife) to be paid up to half of his monthly pay, while he was at sea.

The Seamen's Strike

The National Amalgamated Sailors' and Firemen's Union was founded in 1887, and the Cardiff branch, set up in the following year, had over 6,000 members by 1890. The first successful strike came in 1911 when the union demanded a minimum wage, payment for working overtime, a proper manning scale, a Conciliation Board, and recognition of the union by the Shipping Federation (the owners' organisation). All the seamen's demands were turned down, and so they refused to work.

A month before the strike Edward Tupper ('Captain Tupper') was sent to Cardiff as the union's organiser. The main grievance of the Cardiff men was their low pay, coupled with the recruitment of foreign seamen. In the 1850s foreigners employed on British ships made up 4 per cent of the total workforce, but by the middle of the '80s the figure had risen to nearly 14 per cent, most of whom were German or Scandinavian. Twenty years later foreign seamen made up 30 per cent of those signing on for foreign voyages at Cardiff. The Cardiff men's hostility was directed particularly at the Chinese – there were some Chinese laundries, employing a total of about fifty people, and four licensed boarding-houses with accommodation for just under a hundred, but only about 2 per cent of the seamen signing on at Cardiff were Chinese.

The Cardiff tippers went on strike in sympathy but, as in 1891, the trimmers continued working until six weeks into the strike when a mass meeting in the Cory Hall on 21 July passed a unanimous resolution that 'No trimmer return to work either at Cardiff, Penarth or Barry until the Seamen's Union is recognised by the Shipowners' Federation and also until the police and military are withdrawn'. Cavalry reinforcements had been brought into Maindy Barracks and there was a contingent of Lancashire Fusiliers, as well as a number of Metropolitan Police constables who became particularly disliked – they were mocked and stoned by big crowds, and retaliated with vigorous baton charges.

The employers stationed the *Lady Jocelyn* in Penarth Roads. This vessel, built in 1852, had spent years carrying emigrants, and then mouldered in the London docks as a warehouse for refrigerated meat, until it was taken over by the Shipping Federation as a base for strike-breaking crews. Men could be ferried out by tugboat from Penarth Pier and from Weston, Minehead and Ilfracombe, and one of the union's priorities was to intercept these strike-breakers. In one incident a large group of strikers travelled from Cardiff to Swanbridge, near Sully, and prevented men from setting off for the *Lady Jocelyn*.

There was a good deal of violence during the strike, and tugboat owners' offices were threatened because they had been transporting men out to the *Lady Jocelyn*.

The Chinese laundries and boarding-houses were attacked, and the steamer *Foreric* in Roath Basin was besieged by hundreds when the word got around that some Chinese men had been signed on. A mêlée broke out on board, with the Chinese crew defending themselves with knives and hammers. Police managed to hold the mob back, and order was restored when Tupper arrived. Trouble flared up at another Glasgow-owned ship, the *Annan*, when men from the local workhouse were smuggled in to discharge the cargo. The warehouse they were using was torched, the fire brigade's water hoses were slashed, and the *Annan* was set adrift in the dock. Tupper later appeared in court on charges of unlawful assembly and breach of the peace, but he was acquitted. National talks brought an end to the strike at the beginning of August, with all of the union's demands accepted by the employers.

Vessels

The principal builders of ships at Cardiff in 1880 were listed in the local directory as:

Chapman and Williams (iron) – between the East and West dock basins.
Croft and Dale – West dock.
Davies and Plain – west side of the East Bute dock.
Down and Grant – between the East and West dock basins.
J&M Gunn Ltd – Mount Stuart Graving Dock, Stuart Street.
Charles Hill and Sons (iron and wood) – East and West Bute Graving docks.
Thomas Hodge – dockyard, East Wharf.

Parfitt & Jenkins (iron) – Tubal Cain Works and Roath Dock.
William F. Pile (iron and wood) – East Moors.
William Rees – between the East and West dock basins.

The same source gives the names and office addresses of over forty Cardiff ship owners.

Turnbull's *Register* of 1885 lists sixty-three sailing vessels owned at Cardiff, ranging in size from *David* (12) owned by E.C. Edwards of Grangetown up to the two ships of V. Trayes & Co. – *Canute* (1,215) built in 1869 and *Glenhaven* (1,235) of 1866. Most of those listed in the register – over 75 per cent – were under 200 tons. The largest local sailing fleet was that of W. Brooks: *Forest Princess* (171) 1868; *Forest Queen* (132) 1858; *Mary Elizabeth* (177) 1862; *Nelson Hewertson* (240) 1877; *Rachel Harrison* (88) 1856 and *William Jones* (17) 1877.

Clayton's *Register* of 1865 had listed only three small steam craft at Cardiff. Twenty years later Turnbull's *Register* showed 231 steamships belonging to Cardiff (Newport had 36 and Swansea 31). Thirty of the Cardiff steam vessels were under twenty tons, but at the other end of the scale there were forty of over 1,000 tons, the largest being *Rhodora* (1,763) built in 1881 and owned by F. Edwards. Seventeen of the Cardiff vessels were constructed of iron and one of steel – *Rhiwderin* (737) owned by John Cory, jnr. Many of the Cardiff vessels were owned by single-ship companies.

The census returns provide a snapshot of the shipping in the docks at Penarth and Cardiff on Sunday 3 April 1881. There were around two dozen vessels at Penarth, about half of which were Severn trows and other small sailing craft. There were six steamships, including *Varna, Norfolk, Juan,* and *Scio*. One of the large sailing vessels was the *County of Aberdeen* (1,943), a four-masted iron ship built on the Clyde only two years earlier for R.J. Craig of Glasgow. There were seventeen people on board, including the Chief Mate Alfred Oram (aged thirty-four) and his wife Jane. The crew included seven from Scotland, three from England, and others from New York, Nova Scotia, Ireland and France. On 21 December 1884 the *County of Aberdeen* would leave Cardiff for Bombay, only to disappear on the voyage.

The Cardiff Docks were crammed with 350 vessels, of all sorts, some with full crews on board, others with only a boy or watchman to keep an eye on things. There were about a hundred foreign vessels of which forty or so were French, mostly from Brittany, twenty were from Italy and seven from the United States: *Alexander, City of Brooklyn, Lucile, Niphon, North American, Patrician,* and *William H. Marcy*. The other foreign vessels came from the Adriatic, Denmark, Finland, Germany, Greece, Malta, Norway, Russia and Sweden. The census enumerators visited around fifty steam-powered vessels of all sizes, including the little Penarth ferryboat *La Belle Marie*, tugboats, dredgers, excursion steamers, and Martin and Marquand's *Earl of Roseberry* (1,163).

Twenty or so of the craft present on that Sunday were Severn trows. The Severn Sea was home to a host of trows and other small sailing craft, including sloops and ketches (with crews of three or four) which were the general carriers of the region. Some of the trows at Cardiff on 3 April 1881 were:

Alma. Built in 1854 at Gloucester, and registered there. Crew: William Windows (aged 28); William Hall (30). Both born at Bedminster, Bristol.

Ark. Built in 1841 in Cheshire; registered at Bridgwater. Crew: George Trunks (34),

43 The *County of Haddington*, an iron ship (1,943 gross registered tons, 85.6m long), was built on the Clyde in 1879 by Barclay, Curle & Co. In 1881 the vessel left Penarth with a cargo of coal, but returned for repairs after a severe gale in the Bristol Channnel. Her sister-ship *County of Aberdeen* (built in 1878) was also at Penarth in 1881. On 21 December 1884 the *County of Aberdeen* sailed from Cardiff for Bombay and disappeared on the voyage.

Richard Smith (26), Alfred Luckes (13) – all of Bridgwater.

Brothers. Built in 1847 at Brimscombe, on the Stroudwater Canal in Gloucestershire; registered at Gloucester. Crew: Daniel Gower (26), of Longney, Gloucestershire, his wife Clara (27) and their daughter Minnie (3), John Hookings (21), Taunton; Orlando Silvey (16), Epney, Glos; Henry Sanford (18), Cambridge, Glos.

Electric. Built in 1871 at Barnstaple, by William Westacott; registered at Bridgwater. Crew: John Nicholas (45), William Cridland (37), William Flea (19) – all of Watchet.

Charles Cumper (37) of Beachley.

Elizabeth Anne. Built in 1853 at Polruan and registered at Bridgwater. Crew: Edward Perkins (31), Tom Webber (27), Richard Riddler (24) – all of Porlock.

Flower of Severn. Built at Lydney in 1841; registered at Bristol. Crew: George Guy (41), James Guy (24) – both born at Frampton-on-Severn; William Guy (16), Clifton, Bristol; John Collier (24), Oldbury, Gloucestershire; Noah Bideford Barenger (62), also of Oldbury.

Good Intent. Built in 1790 at Plymouth; registered at Bridgwater. Crew: William Smart (44) – owner; Frederick Smart (20), James Smart (17) – all of Bridgwater.

Hannah. Built in 1872 at Framilode, Gloucestershire; registered at Gloucester. Crew: Charles Lawrence (63) of Saul; Francis Silvey (40) of Bristol, Henry Hall of Bridgwater.

Longney Lass. Built in 1842 at Bridgnorth, Shropshire; registered at Gloucester. Crew: Henry Evans (56) and John Hill (50) of Frampton-on-Severn; Thomas Bence (50), Bristol.

Neptune. Built in 1863 at Gloucester, and registered there. Crew: John Petheram (36), Gatcombe, Glos; Richard Trayhen (36), Beachley; William Petheram (17), Aure.

Prudence. Built in 1822 near Ironbridge, Shropshire; registered at Gloucester. Crew: James Cook (44), Framilode; John Birt, Epney and Thomas Collier (32), Framilode.

Theodore. Built in 1871 at Saul; registered at Gloucester. Crew: Francis Heale (25), Framilode; John Woodward (29), Highbridge, Somerset and John Butler (32), Bideford, Devonshire.

These small sailing vessels could still compete with steam in providing a flexible and convenient cargo-carrying service between local ports, and at the beginning of the 1880s there were far more UK sailing vessels than steam: sailing vessels: 19,325 (total tonnage 3,688,000); steam vessels: 5,505 (total tonnage 3,004,000). There were some routes where big sailing ships provided an alternative to steamships – one was to Australia, and in 1883 the *Cutty Sark*, carrying a cargo of wool, sailed from Australia to Britain, including rounding Cape Horn, in eighty-two days. Another was the voyage from Europe around Cape Horn, to collect guano or nitrate from Chile, a typical voyage being to take coal from Britain to Valparaiso, then continue up the coast in ballast to take on nitrate, probably at Iquique, the most important port, where there could be a hundred vessels waiting for their cargo. A barquentine, sailing from the Bristol Channel to Iquique, would take about seventy-two to ninety days to get there. One who made this voyage was the future Poet Laureate, John Masefield. At the age of thirteen he had joined the training ship HMS *Conway*, which was permanently moored on the River Mersey. In April 1894 – aged nearly sixteen – he went to sea, as an apprentice, in the *Gilcruix* (2,304). Built in 1886 at Whitehaven, this was a four-masted iron barque owned by the White Star Line. John Masefield, joining at Cardiff, was one of a crew of thirty-three (including six apprentices, five of whom were 'old Conways') making the voyage around Cape Horn. They left Cardiff on 25 April, carrying a cargo of patent fuel, the young apprentice soon becoming sea-sick. Going aloft in the 'roaring forties' he described the wind as having 'a fervour and fury' which took his breath away, the sail threshing about and the mast bending under the strain.

Rounding Cape Horn the deck and rigging became covered in ice, which also tore a hole in the ship's hull. They arrived at Iquique in the first week of August, thirteen weeks after leaving Cardiff. John Masefield fell ill and was certified as a 'Distressed British Seaman' by the British Consul, which meant that he could be sent back to Britain by steamship. He left the *Gilcruix* on 29 August 1894 and after spending some time in the British Hospital in Valparaiso, arrived home at Ledbury by the end of October. (The *Gilcruix* was sold to a Hamburg firm in June 1895 and re-named *Barmbek*. At the start of the First World War the barque was detained by a French cruiser, towed to Brest, sold to a local company, and renamed *Pacifique*. After a collision with an American steamer in March 1921, off the Isle of Wight, the vessel was towed to Le Havre and then to a breaker's yard at Caen).

Another sailing ship, the *Great Britain*, left Penarth for San Francisco on 6 February 1886. Eighty years later the vessel was brought back to Bristol, where it had been built in 1843 by the Great Western Steamship Company under the supervision of I.K. Brunel and others. The vessel was originally to be a paddle steamer, but an iron propeller was installed after the company's directors were impressed by the performance of the *Archimedes*. At the time of the launch the *Great Britain,* a steamer rigged as a six-masted schooner, was easily the largest ship in the world and was designed to carry 250 passengers and 130 crew across the Atlantic. Her maiden voyage from Liverpool to New York began on 26 July 1845, and took fifteen days.

Great Britain ran aground at Dundrum Bay in 1846, and was then sold to Gibbs, Bright and Company of Liverpool. The ship was modified so as to be able to carry 750 passengers, and her appearance was changed, so that there were now two funnels and four masts. *Great Britain* began a new career carrying migrants to Australia, a trade which was to be stimulated by the discovery of gold in 1851. After the first voyage another mast was taken away, leaving three, all carrying square sails.

For well over twenty years the great ship ploughed backwards and forwards between Britain and Australia, taking about two months in each direction – under sail for long periods, using steam power only when necessary. There were occasional diversions such as a government charter to transport army units to the Crimea, and to India after the Mutiny.

Following the Crimean War more changes were made, including alterations to the positions of the masts and removing a funnel. In the late 1870s the engines were taken out, and the *Great Britain* began a new life as a three-masted sailing ship, taking Welsh coal around Cape Horn to San Francisco. On the final voyage – from Penarth – she was forced to seek refuge at the Falkland Islands, where the vessel was sold and used as a hulk for storing coal and wool. Derelict, the *Great Britain* was eventually rescued and brought in triumph up the Avon to Bristol on 19 July 1970, completing the voyage begun at Penarth in 1886.

The *Denbigh Castle* was a three-masted ship built on the Clyde as the *Marathon* in 1893. In 1908, owned by Robert Thomas (now of Liverpool, but originally from Nefyn on the Llyn Peninsula) the vessel spent eight-and-a-half months continuously at sea, taking over a year to carry a cargo of patent fuel from Cardiff to Mollendo, on the west coast of South America. *Denbigh Castle* left Cardiff on 9 October 1908, towed by steam tug as far as Lundy. Two months later the vessel approached Cape Horn, was still there on Christmas Day and still there in March – all the while battling against atrocious weather.

With food stocks running low, the master decided to take his battered vessel to Australia, arriving at Fremantle in June 1909, after 253 days at sea. Some of the crew mutinied, but the ship was able to leave on 5 July, arriving at Mollendo (described as 'a few houses and huts, mostly huts') on 21 November 1909. Two of Robert Thomas's other vessels were already there – *Westfield* and *Dolbadarn Castle*. After another mutiny, the *Denbigh Castle* set sail for Europe with a cargo of guano, arriving at Antwerp after a passage of 130 days. The *Shipping Gazette* (12 August 1910) commented that the *Denbigh Castle*:

Homeward bound from the west coast of America, is now four months out...To recall the details of the round voyage of this ship since she sailed from Cardiff on 9 October 1908, is to emphasize the ill-luck that may befall a vessel dependent solely on the wind for propulsion... Practically speaking the *Denbigh Castle* is taking about two years for a round voyage to the west coast of America and home again to the United Kingdom... It will be noted that on nearly every stage of the voyage the *Denbigh Castle* has been overdue.

44 The *Denbigh Castle* was built on the Clyde (as the *Marathon*) in 1893. On 9 October 1908 the ship set off from Cardiff with a cargo of patent fuel intended for Mollendo, in Peru. *Denbigh Castle* spent over eight months continuously at sea, arriving at Fremantle in June 1909. Five months later the vessel finally dropped anchor at Mollendo.

Steamships

A typical cargo steamer built in the period immediately before the First World War was about 114m long x 16m broad, with a hold depth of 8m, and around 4,500 gross registered tons. The vessel was powered by quadruple-expansion engines, which consumed just under seventy tons of coal a day, and there were five cargo holds, each accessed through a hatch. The vessel was unlikely to have a radio. In May 1897 Guglielmo Marconi had managed to send Morse radio messages across water for the first time – between Flat Holm and Lavernock Point, near Penarth – and by 1914 the number of merchant ships, of all nations, able to send and receive radio messages had grown to about 2,500. This was only a small proportion of the total, as the United Kingdom alone had over 21,000 registered vessels.

In 1914, nearly 70 per cent of the ocean going steam vessels registered in the UK were *tramp ships* (as opposed to *liners* which ran regular services, to a timetable, between specified ports) and nearly all Cardiff steamers were of that kind, tramping the world for trade – in the early days the vessels were sometimes referred to as *seekers*, looking for cargoes from anywhere. The owner provided the vessel for the charterer's cargo and the ship sailed when it was ready. The terms agreed between the ship's owner and the charterer were set out in a document known as a *charter party*, of which there were three common types:

Voyage. The ship was chartered from the owner at an agreed *freight rate*, and the charterer was responsible for arranging for the cargo, and for its handling.

Time. The owner was paid for a voyage according to time, either monthly or at the end of the voyage.

Demise. The charterer, rather than the owner, was responsible for maintaining the vessel and paying all charges incurred.

Freight rates were determined by the interaction of the supply of and demand for vessels on the worldwide market. Freight rates fluctuated, and when they dropped too far could lead to vessels being operated at a loss, scrapped, or laid up until the market conditions changed. From around 1880, demand for shipping remained at a fairly high level, but freight rates dipped in 1883 and from 1884 too many vessels were available for the volume of trade. Three years later freights improved, but were depressed again in the early 1890s. The wars in South Africa led to an increased demand for ships, and a rise in freight rates in the final years of the century, but the 1900s brought a worldwide depression to the shipping industry, which came to an end with the beginning of the First World War.

Cardiff Steamship Enterprises Started 1888–1914

Dozens of new steamship companies appeared at Cardiff. They included:

Neale & West. Not tramp-ship owners, but fishing fleet operators, Neale and West's trawlers were a familiar sight at Cardiff for nearly seventy years. Joshua Neale and Henry West, fish merchants in Custom House Street, bought the Hull trawler *Lark* (52) so that they might have a more regular supply of fish – that was in 1888. By 1906 Neale and West owned nineteen steam trawlers, based on the Bute West Dock. Just as Neale and West had gone fishing to secure their supplies, so they entered ice-making, setting up the Cardiff Ice & Cold Storage Co. By the time Henry West took his leave of the company in 1910, to concentrate on the ice-making, they were also operating trawlers out of Milford Haven.

Before the First World War Neale and West trawlers were going as far as the coast of North Africa in their search for hake, mostly fishing from large modern vessels. Neale and West had been involved in training Japanese fishermen, and decided to name most of their new acquisitions after places in Japan: in 1911 the fleet was joined by *Ijuin*, *Kudama*, *Miura*, and *Nodzu*.

J.T. Duncan. John Thomas Duncan, from Glasgow, worked in shipping offices in Cardiff before setting up as a ship-broker. With his partner Jacques Valette he formed a single-ship company in 1889 to buy the nine-year-old *Benefactor* (1,034), which had been built at Liverpool by W.H. Potter & Son. Valette left after six years, the enterprise was re-titled 'J. T. Duncan & Co'. and the twelve-year-old *Stokesley* (1,047) was acquired. Both vessels traded to France. By 1914 the company owned five steamers.

Chellew Steam Navigation Co. Chellews had an office in Cardiff, although the vessels were registered at Falmouth, in the home county of the Line's founders. William Chellew and his son Richard started their career as steamship owners by running the *City of Truro* and the *Duke of Cornwall*, and by the 1890s they had five single-ship companies and a base at Cardiff. Richard Chellew became a director of several other enterprises, including the Mount Stuart Dry Dock Co. Chellew vessels traded to the Mediterranean, the Black Sea, South America and India.

W.J. Tatem. The eighteen-year-old William James Tatem of Appledore arrived in Cardiff in 1886 to take up a clerical job with Anning Brothers, where he was to stay for ten years, learning about the management of trading vessels.

Tatem set up his own single-ship company with the new *Lady Lewis* (2,950), built at Stockton-on-Tees by Richardson, Duck & Co. and named after the wife of the manager of the Bute Docks. Launched on 17 June 1897, the master for her first eight voyages was William Reardon Smith. New ships followed at yearly intervals (the first fourteen all built by Richardson, Duck) – 1898: *Sir W.T Lewis* (3,517), named after the Docks manager; 1899: *Shandon* (3,850); 1900: *Chulmleigh* (3,997), *Southport* (3,588) and *Westward Ho* (3,596). The *Wooda* (3,804) of 1901 was destined to run aground at least four times, at Baltimore in August 1901 and in the Black Sea in September and December 1905, and again in September 1911. Two of Tatem's ships were lost with all hands, *Lady Lewis* in 1906 and *Dulverton* in April 1907.

As the size of the fleet grew, so did the size of the ships and in 1905 Tatem's took delivery of the *Wellington* (5,600) and the *Torrington* (5,597) which were both turret ships

45 Tatem's *Chorley* (3,828) in the Cardiff Channel Dry Docks. Launched in August 1901 by Richardson, Duck & Co., Stockton-on-Tees, Tatem's sold the vessel in 1916. It was to be torpedoed and sunk off Start Point on 22 March 1917.

(see *Edward Nicholl*, below) built by Doxford and Sons of Sunderland. In her first year of service the *Torrington* was badly damaged in a collision; two years later she grounded in the River Elbe and was crashed into by three vessels in succession, but survived, to continue tramping.

Owen and Watkin Williams. Brought up on the Llyn peninsula in north Wales, Owen worked in a ship-owner's office, while Watkin became a Master Mariner. In 1895 they took their first steps into ship-owning with *Hesperides* (2,404), built in 1884 to carry meat from South America. A single-ship company was formed to finance the vessel's refit as a tramp steamer, with the largest investors in the enterprise being Owen Williams £750, Watkin Williams £500, and their uncle Griffith Williams who put up £1,000. *Hesperides* was lost on 10 October 1897, on passage from Santiago de Cuba to Baltimore with iron ore.

The *Hesperides* was replaced by the *Silurian* (940) in 1898, straight from the yard of R. Craggs & Son of Middlesbrough. Three vessels were bought in 1900: *Canganian* (1,143), *Demetian* (1,108), and *Ordovician* (1,112), and four more in 1901: *Venodotian* (1,168), *Segontian* (1,171), *Goidelian* (1,220), and *Coranian* (1,223).

On 24 June 1905 the *Goidelian* (en route from Gandia to Liverpool with fruit and general cargo) sank after hitting rocks off the coast of Portugal – all of the crew were saved. On 3 October 1907 *Mervinian* was carrying coal from Swansea to Marseille when she foundered in the Bay of Biscay with the loss of five men.

Owen and Watkin Williams added to their portfolio of companies by establishing the 'Golden Cross Line' which was to provide a liner service to Mediterranean ports, but this did not diminish their general tramping business. The ten vessels in their fleet at the outbreak of the First World War ranged in size from the *Silurian* (940) up to *Tavian* (4,567).

Edward Nicholl, a Cornishman from Redruth, became a Great Western Railway apprentice at Swindon, before being employed as chief engineer on the *Gwenllian Thomas*, Evan Thomas Radcliffe's first vessel. In 1884 he was appointed marine superintendent for Thomas and Radcliffe and then for W. & C.T. Jones. At the age of forty-one he took up ship-owning, forming the Cardiff Hall Line.

In 1904 he bought the first *turret ship* to be owned at Cardiff. A turret ship was constructed with a raised deck above the main hull. This elevated part was, usually, about half as wide as the ship's beam. The deck at the top of the main hull was known as the 'harbour deck' and could be used for deck cargo such as timber. (A turret ship is shown in illustration 52 on page 113). The advantage of these vessels was that they attracted lower harbour and Suez Canal charges. It was claimed, in addition, that they were cheaper to construct than traditional ships, and that the handling of some bulk cargoes was easier. The first turret ship was built in 1892, the last in 1911 by which time 176 had come down the Doxford slipways at Sunderland. The years of peak production were 1904–7, when more than eighty were built. Edward Nicholl bought six: 1904 *Whateley Hall* (3,712) and *Eaton Hall* (3,711), 1906 *Tredegar Hall* (3,764), 1907 *Silksworth Hall* (4,777), 1908 *Haigh Hall* (4,809) and *Grindon Hall* (3,712). Seven new turret ships were bought by other Cardiff owners between 1905 and 1908. After this only nine more such vessels were built, killed off by changes in the way port and Canal dues were calculated.

In the post-war shipping boom half-a-dozen ageing turret ships were bought by Cardiff owners.

Edward Nicholl's *Grindon Hall* (3,721) – only two years old – was lost in December 1907 on a voyage carrying barley and maize from the Romanian port of Sulina to the Clyde.

In the years before the First World War Nicholl was managing eleven vessels, including *Welbeck Hall* (2,760) and *Haigh Hall* (4,809).

W.H. Seager. William Seager began business as a Cardiff ships' chandler in 1892. 'W. H. Seager & Co'. was formed in 1904 to manage *Tempus* (2,981), which worked the routes to the River Plate, the Mediterranean and the Black Sea. At the start of the First World War the fleet consisted of *Tempus* (2,981) built in 1904; *Salvus* (2,259) built 1904; *Campus* (3,695) built 1911 and *Amicus* (3,695) built 1911.

William Reardon Smith. Another West Country immigrant to Cardiff was W.R. Smith, who was at sea in local Appledore craft from the age of twelve, gaining his Master's certificate at the age of twenty-five. Among the vessels he commanded were the barque *Drumadoon* and, in the early 1890s, the steamship *Baron Douglas* (2,500), both owned by H. Hogarth & Sons.

In 1897 William Smith was appointed as the first master of Tatem's first ship, the *Lady Lewis*, in which he took coal to the River Plate and brought grain back to Europe. He then took charge of the same owner's new vessel, the *Shandon*. Retiring from the sea in 1900 at the age of forty-four, he became a ship-owner five years later in partnership with his son. Their first vessel was the *City of Cardiff* (3,089), ordered from the Ropner yard at Stockton-on-Tees, and placed into the 'Instow Steamship Company'. Although he had been living in Cardiff for some time, and his shipping company was to be managed from there, the vessel was registered at Bideford, as were subsequent ships. The *City of Cardiff* was to be lost in 1912, on the rocks near Land's End. Smith's next purchase was *Leeds City* (4,298) – again from Ropner – in 1908. Both steamers were employed on the usual coal out/grain home round.

Frederick Jones was a Cardiffian, born in Adamsdown. At the age of nineteen he completed his apprenticeship with Parfitt and Jenkins at their Tubal Cain Foundry and went to sea as an engineer. Ten years later he became marine superintendent for Capel & Co. Frederick Jones ventured into ship owning in 1907, when he organised a single-ship company to buy the thirty-year-old *Melrose Abbey* (1,211) from Cardiff owners Pyman Watson. The purchase price of £3,500 was soon raised, with 370 x £10 shares being taken up in the first three months. The vessel was immediately chartered by her former owners for eighteen months, after which her usual voyages were to the French ports or, sometimes, to Lisbon. *Melrose Abbey* was wrecked on 31 July 1909, with no loss of life. Frederick Jones entered the First World War with three vessels: *Tintern Abbey*, *Neath Abbey* and, still on the stocks, *Singleton Abbey*.

The British Antarctic Expedition

The *Terra Nova* sailed from Cardiff on 15 June 1910, seen off by large crowds on shore and with other well-wishers on board the paddle steamers *Devonia* and *Ravenswood*. The British Antarctic Expedition – leader, Captain Robert Falcon Scott, Royal Navy – was finally on its way. The *Terra Nova* (744) was a three-masted wooden sealing vessel built in 1884 by Alexander Stephen at Dundee. *Terra Nova's* voyage from Cardiff was not its first to the Antarctic, as it had been chartered by the Admiralty in 1903 as a relief ship for Scott's earlier expedition. The vessel was sold to the Admiralty in November 1909 for Scott's latest venture. *Terra Nova* had left London on 1 June 1910, Captain Scott disembarked a few miles down the Thames, and the ship carried on to Cardiff, arriving on Friday 10 June.

The *Terra Nova* came to Cardiff because of the level of local support, particularly from the *Western Mail*, the Lord Mayor (Alderman John Chappell), Daniel Radcliffe and other docksmen. At Roath Dock 300 tons of patent fuel, given by the Crown Preserved Coal Company, were taken on board and *Terra Nova* was then moved to the East Dock to receive 100 tons of free coal (half from Insole's and half from the Ynyshir Steam Coal Company). Among the donated stores being stowed were 1,200 bottles of Stone's Ginger Wine. The expedition members were entertained well in Cardiff, with theatre visits, dinners, and accommodation.

At 1.00p.m. on 15 June 1910 *Terra Nova* was towed out, with a party of local big-wigs on board. A multitude watched as the vessel moved down channel, accompanied by a flotilla including W.H. Tuke's tugboat *Lady Morgan*. Spectators were packed on

46 Departure day for the *Terra Nova* and the British Antarctic Expedition, 15 June 1910.

to *Devonia* and *Ravenswood* each of which had a band playing. Near the Breaksea Lightship the official Cardiff party transferred from *Terra Nova* to the tug *Falcon* as did Captain Scott who – still trying to raise funds – did not leave Britain until a month later. He and his wife travelled to South Africa in HMS *Saxon*, arriving at Cape Town on 2 August. This voyage of just over two weeks may be compared with that of the rest of the expedition on *Terra Nova*, which took over two months to get to Cape Town, leaking, and with all on board taking turns at the pumps. The vessel was put into dry dock in New Zealand in the hope of stopping the leaks, at last entering the pack ice on 9 December 1910. The men who were to reach the Pole a month after Roald Amundsen would not return: Scott, Bowers, Evans, Oates and Wilson.

Amundson lectured in Cardiff on 3 December 1912 on 'How I reached the Pole,' but the fate of Scott's party was not known in Britain until two months later.

Three years after leaving Cardiff the *Terra Nova* returned (on 14 June 1913), to be met by Scott's widow, his son and, later, a group including John Chappell and Daniel Radcliffe. The next day, a Sunday, thousands of people came, many by special train, to see the *Terra Nova*. The vessel remained in port for another two months, the crew was paid off and Bowring Brothers, exercising their option, bought the ship back. *Terra Nova* left on 15 August 1913, after a refit, returning to work around the Labrador and Newfoundland coasts. Nearly thirty years later, in September 1943, the vessel sank off Greenland. All the crew survived.

Some Local Ships Lost 1900–14

During this period of depressed freight rates the value of vessels dropped, often to below their insured value, and a ship could be worth more lying on the bed of the ocean than steaming on its surface. A number of Cardiff ships were lost in suspicious circumstances, to the financial benefit of the owners, and Cardiff ship-owners built up such a bad reputation that they had to pay higher rates of insurance than owners in other ports. Another practice which developed at this time was for people to take out insurances on vessels in which they had no other interest, and when the *Albion* sank in 1908 it was found that nearly £12,000 worth of insurance had been taken out by a number of individuals. These insurance policies were, in effect, 'bets' about the survival of the vessel, and were to be banned by the *Marine Insurance (Gambling) Act* which became law on 20 October 1909.

Some of the Cardiff vessels lost (not necessarily in suspicious circumstances) in these years before the First World War were:

Aberporth: Sank in the Black Sea, June 1905.

Lady Lewis: Tatem's first vessel, built in 1897, was lost on the coast of Argentina on a voyage from Bahia Blanca to Barcelona, April 1906.

Prairie Flower: The boiler of this Cardiff tug exploded in Penarth Roads, killing a member of the crew, May 1906.

Dulverton: Owned by W.J. Tatem, disappeared on passage between Bahia Blanca and Antwerp, April 1907.

Powis: Sank in the Aegean, June 1907, carrying a cargo of iron ore.

Mervinian: Sank after a collision off Gibraltar. Six men were drowned, October 1907.

Grindon Hall: Disappeared in the Black Sea, December 1907.

Kirkwall: Sank after a collision in the North Sea in August 1908. Twenty people lost their lives.

Verajean: A three-masted ship built at Dumbarton in 1891. Blown on to Rhoose Point on 1 September 1908, the vessel was pulled off ten days later by the tug *Lady of the Isles,* but was sent to be broken up at Briton Ferry.

Torridge: Owned by W.J. Tatem, wrecked at the Seychelles on a voyage from Port Natal to Galle (Ceylon) in April 1910.

British Standard: Lost off the coast of Brazil, May 1910.

Wimbourne. Rotterdam to Barry, in ballast. Wrecked near Land's End, 7 November 1910.

Hatfield: Collision off the Kent coast. Only one crew member was saved (out of nineteen), October 1911.

Cardiff City: Six years old, and on voyage in ballast from Le Havre to Cardiff. Ended up on the rocks of Mill Bay, near Land's End. All crew members were rescued by breeches buoy, 1912.

Alum Chine: Owned by Harper & Co. Destroyed by an explosion in port at Baltimore, Maryland. The vessel was loading 350 tons of dynamite, intended for use in building the Panama Canal. *Alum Chine* sank and a tugboat was destroyed, as were two barges which were taking railway wagons to the ship. Thirty-three people were killed and sixty injured, March 1913.

W.W. Jones: a Cardiff pilot cutter which sank after a collision, May 1914.

47 *Verajean* aground at Rhoose Point in September 1908. Towed off ten days later, the vessel had to be broken up at Briton Ferry.

On the Eve of the First World War

South Wales miners produced over 46,000,000 tons of coal. 439 men were killed by an underground explosion at Senghennydd in October 1913.

There were 113 coal exporting businesses in Cardiff alone. Barry, Cardiff and Penarth sent abroad a total of 22,108,000 tons of coal in 1913.

Clearances of vessels carrying cargo from Cardiff were: *Coastal clearances:* Sail 1,732 (tonnage 174,297); Steam 6,092 (tonnage 2,033,175). *Foreign clearances:* Sail 291 (tonnage 162,648); Steam 6,216 (tonnage 10,019,175).

There were around seventy Cardiff tramp-ship-owning firms, managing about 320 vessels.

The five largest firms in 1914 were: Evan Thomas Radcliffe with twenty-eight ships; John Cory – nineteen; Chellew – eighteen; W.J. Tatem – seventeen; W. & C.T. Jones – fifteen. Morel, Edward Nicholl, Owen & Watkin Williams and Reardon Smith had ten vessels each. Neale and West owned nineteen trawlers, one of which was responsible for providing Cardiff with its most fondly remembered attraction, Billy the Seal.

Accidentally caught in the net of a trawler in 1912, Billy was put into the lake at Victoria Park (which then had a small menagerie) and entertained visitors with his antics until he died in 1939 (when Billy was found to be a 'she').

48 Shipping at Cardiff.

8

THE GREAT WAR

4 August 1914: Kronstadt. On the day the war began Frederick Jones's *Tintern Abbey* was at Kronstadt, near St Petersburg, unloading coal for the Russian navy. Jones's thirteen-year-old son was on board. Unable to risk a Baltic Sea dominated by the German navy, the ship and crew were stranded. After three months of idleness it was decided that *Tintern Abbey* would be left at St Petersburg in the care of the master and one crew member, and the rest would try to get home. They set off, crossing Finland, Sweden and Norway, using any transport they could find – including horse and cart. Reaching Bergen at last, they found a steamer bound for the Tyne. *Tintern Abbey* lay at St Petersburg for over three years, but the vessel was allowed to leave after the revolution of 1917, manned by a neutral Swedish crew. It was taken to Bergen and then, with a British crew, sailed for Bristol with a cargo of timber, arriving in time for New Year 1918. For the final months of the war *Tintern Abbey* was chartered as an Admiralty collier. In 1921 she returned to Russia, having been sold to the All-Russia Co-operative Society and renamed *Jacov Sverdlov.*

4 August 1914: Cardiff. The Docks were now guarded by soldiers and policemen, as priority was given to the loading of coal for the Royal Navy. The *Western Mail* told its readers that the Admiralty agents were 'taking up steamers freely… and loading operations on Admiralty account were heavy… steamers in some cases arriving, loading and sailing in less than twenty-four hours'. Fifty-six German vessels in British waters were seized: twenty-two sailing vessels and thirty-four steamships. Detained at Cardiff were the ship *Schwarzenburg,* the steamers *Carl* and *Chile,* and the *R.C. Rickmers* – a five-masted auxiliary-powered steel barque, built at Bremerhaven in 1906. Her cargo of grain had been discharged and she was about to load coal. Renamed *Neath,* the vessel was sunk off Fastnet, on 27 March 1917, by the German submarine U-66.

By 20 August 2,578 people had registered as aliens at the Cardiff Law Courts, among them 275 Greeks, 265 Russians and 213 Germans. Most of the German men had been lodged in Cardiff Castle, but were later marched through the pouring rain to the Seamen's Institute on Bute Street. Many of the detainees were young cadets from the *R.C. Rickmers* – 'all of well-to-do parents' according to the *Western Mail.* Members of the local clergy visited the Institute, and the inmates were entertained by lectures, illustrated with 'magic lantern' slides. Twelve German wives and eight children were lodged in the workhouse.

4 August 1914: Savona. Tatem's three-year-old *Braunton* (4,575) was destined for a long wait at this Italian port, because the stevedores were on strike, then the First World War broke out and the German crew members left for home. The ship was eventually able to leave for Baltimore, Maryland, where grain was loaded for Bordeaux. At Bordeaux the crew kicked their heels for a month before being ordered to take their ship to St Nazaire, where the grain cargo was discharged. Returning to Barry, *Braunton* was converted into an Admiralty collier and sent off to the Pacific in support of a naval squadron, passing through the Panama Canal only six months after its opening. *Braunton* returned to Liverpool in June 1915 with a cargo of Cuban sugar, before being sent off to Newfoundland to collect pit props, which were destined for Cardiff. After further trips to La Spezia and Port Said, Nova Scotia and Philadelphia, the *Braunton* was torpedoed off Beachy Head on 7 April 1916.

Losses of ships such as the *Braunton* exacerbated the already severe shortage of shipping. In the first six months of the war seventy British merchant ships and thirty-six trawlers were lost, and by March 1915 at least three enemy submarines were prowling around the Irish Sea and the approaches to the Bristol Channel. On 27/28 March U-28 sank four vessels around Lundy and The Smalls. On 7 May the Cunard liner *Lusitania* was torpedoed off the Old Head of Kinsale, with the loss of 1,200 lives. Nearly fifty vessels were sunk in the Western Approaches during June and July, losses which jeopardised the efforts being made by the British to support their Allies by sending food, fuel and munitions to France, Italy and Russia. Providing ships to transport British troops was a major concern: a constant flow of reinforcements had to be taken to France, and moving three army divisions to Gallipoli took fifty steamships in March and April 1915.

Almost all British merchant ships were requisitioned for the duration of the war, with their owners being retained to manage them, and the Cardiff firm of Mathwin played an important part in acquiring coal-carrying vessels for the Admiralty. Three or four cargoes of coal a month were sent to Egypt (where there were Australian, British, Canadian, Indian and New Zealand troops), and from March 1915 between thirty and fifty ships a month went to France. From February 1917 the coal to France was transported in convoys, with 'assembly points' at Southend, St Helens (Isle of Wight), Portland and Penzance.

To keep the sea lanes clear 250 civilian vessels had been called-up in the first month of the war for conversion to the minesweeping role. They included all of Neale and West's trawlers, ten of which would be sunk. The local paddle-steamers were also fitted out as minesweepers and sustained casualties: *Lady Ismay* was lost on 2 December 1914 and the *Brighton Queen* hit a mine off Nieuport on 6 October 1915, with the loss of seven lives. The *Barry* operated out of Troon, and was later to ferry soldiers at Gallipoli.

Because of delays on the railways and a decline in coasting trade, south Wales' ports drew an increasing bunkering trade – ships taking on coal to fuel their own boilers – and became the main centre for this, causing further congestion. The United States entered the war in April 1917, soon becoming aware of the difficulties of supplying coal to its forces in Europe. A fleet of US naval vessels was allocated to the task with the first ship, USS *Bath*, leaving Cardiff on 5 October 1917 carrying 3,300 tons of coal. A headquarters was set up at the Angel Hotel, Cardiff, which was transformed into the United States Ship *Chatinouka* and by November 1918 there were about 6,000 US Navy personnel involved in the operation, with US Marines guarding facilities at Cardiff Docks. The coal supply voyages continued well into 1919, by now using vessels newly built in America, many of them with the name 'Lake' (for example, *Lake Bloomington, Lake Charlotte, Lake Clear, Lake Conesus, Lake Crescent, Lake Gaspar, Lake*

ZEICHNET
KRIEGS-ANLEIHE
FÜR U-BOOTE GEGEN
ENGLAND

49 A First World War poster exhorts people to support a war-loan to finance U-boats. The British Isles surrounded by German submarines makes the aim clear.

Yahara). Two months after the Armistice one of these vessels, the USS *Lake Erie* (2,028) built at Detroit in 1917, collided with the *Hazel Branch*, a British steamship, and sank off Lavernock Point. There were no casualties. *Lake Erie* was a 'Standard Ship,' one of a large number ordered from the United States by the British Shipping Controller. When the United States entered the war, all those still being built, including *War Beaver*, which was renamed *Lake Erie*, were requisitioned by the US government for its own use. The vessel was raised from the sea seven months after sinking and sold to Norwegian owners in November 1919, later operating under the names *Gezina*, *Ragni*, *Arpeco* and *Force* before being broken up in 1959.

50 The *War Beaver* was a wartime 'Standard Ship', one of many ordered by Britain, but requisitioned by the American government when the US entered the war. Built at Detroit in 1917, the vessel was renamed USS *Lake Erie* in January 1918. On 16 January 1919 she sank after colliding with the British steamship *Hazel Branch*, off Lavernock Point, near Penarth. *Lake Erie* was salvaged in the August and sold in November 1919, trading for another forty years before being broken up.

Losses: 1914–18

The British merchant fleet was to be greatly depleted by the war. Most of the vessels were destroyed by submarines or mines but some were victims of surface raiders. One of these, the light cruiser *Karlsruhe*, searched for prey in the Caribbean and South Atlantic during the first three months of the war, accounting for over a dozen merchant vessels including, on 21 September 1914, Reardon Smith's *Cornish City* (3,816). Built as the *Charlton* in 1906, she had been bought by the Cardiff firm in 1912. On her way from Barry to Rio de Janeiro (with 5,500 tons of coal) *Cornish City* was sunk some 250 miles off the coast of Brazil, where the crew was later landed. This was the first Cardiff-owned ship to be lost in the war.

The *Emden*, another light cruiser, was sent off to patrol the Indian Ocean, where she was responsible for disposing of a Russian cruiser, a French destroyer and sixteen British merchant ships, including Tatem's *Exford* (4,542). The Cardiff vessel was taking 5,000 tons of coal to India, when she was unfortunate enough to encounter the *Emden,* which seized *Exford* as a prize. On 11 December 1914 the *Exford* was retaken by the British Armed Merchant Cruiser *Himalaya*. Another Cardiff victim fell to the converted merchant ship *Mowe*. Built as the *Pungo* (for carrying bananas) at Geestemunde, she was launched on 9 May 1914 and commissioned into the German navy on 1 November 1914. The *Mowe* could assume various guises: guns were out of sight, a false funnel could be put up, the height of the masts could be altered and the outline of the superstructure changed. *Corbridge* (3,687) was captured on 11 January 1916, and taken to the mouth of the Amazon, where she remained until *Mowe* returned on 27 January. All the coal was transferred to the cruiser – a task which took three days – and *Corbridge* was then scuttled.

The most unusual German surface raider was the *Seeadler* (Sea Eagle) – a full-rigged steel sailing ship, launched in 1888 as the *Pass of Balmaha* by Robert Duncan at Port Glasgow. Now the *Seeadler*, she set sail from Bremerhaven as a commerce raider, disguised as a Norwegian vessel, and equipped with concealed guns and an auxiliary engine. The hold had been fitted with rows of bunks – enough to accommodate 400 prisoners. The six-year-old *Horngarth* (3,609), owned by Turnbull Brothers of Cardiff, was sighted on 11 March 1917, carrying a cargo of maize from Montevideo to Plymouth. Captain Felix von Luckner decided that *Seeadler* should appear as a ship on fire, so smoke was made and distress flares fired, causing the Cardiff vessel to alter course to help. The sailing ship then unfurled the German ensign, the victim's wireless aerials were shot away, the crew taken off, and the *Horngarth* was sunk by explosives. This German raider sank a total of fifteen vessels, before being wrecked in the Pacific on 2 August 1917 – the crew and their prisoners were rescued.

A U-boat's preferred method of attack was to find a lone merchant ship, come to the surface, and then sink the target by gunfire or explosive charges. Tatem's *Torridge* (5,036) was lost in this way on 6 September 1916 forty miles off Start Point, although all the crew members were rescued. A 'Q' ship was a British merchant vessel acting as a decoy to encourage this kind of attack. When a submarine appeared a 'panic party' would row away from the 'Q' ship, trying to give the impression that the vessel had been abandoned. In fact, crew members were still on board, manning the hidden guns. When the submarine was close enough, up went the White Ensign, and the guns fired. During the war over 200 vessels served as 'Q' vessels, sinking about fifteen enemy craft.

Evan Thomas Radcliffe's *Dunraven* (3,117) – formerly *Boverton* – served in the 'Q' role. On 8 August 1917 the Cardiff ship was fired on by a surfaced U-boat, U-71, in a position about 130 miles south-west of Ushant. Captain Gordon Campbell VC sent off the panic boat while other sailors stayed on board, but the Germans saw the *Dunraven*'s guns, and U-71 dived. Another panic boat set off, hoping to entice the submarine to the surface again. The *Dunraven* was hit by torpedoes, and a third panic boat left the ship, although two guns were still manned. U-71 surfaced, fired again, and dived. Two torpedoes launched by *Dunraven* missed. The U-boat decided to call it a day, and left. Her intended victim was still afloat, but one man had been killed. The *Dunraven* sank while being towed towards Plymouth. Two Victoria Crosses were awarded by ballot to Lieutenant C.G. Bonner and Petty Officer E.H. Pitcher.

Reardon Smith's *Bradford City* (3,683) also operated as a 'Q' vessel from 1915 until sunk in August 1917 by the Austro-Hungarian submarine U-28 , off the Italian coast. As it became more common for merchant vessels to be armed, and because of the activities of 'Q' ships, U-boats changed their tactics and made their initial attack with torpedoes. The numbers of German submarines increased from twenty-eight in December 1914 to well over a hundred by February 1917, the month in which the Germans declared 'unrestricted submarine warfare' and Allied losses increased dramatically – during April 1917 (the month when the United States became a combatant) of every four ships leaving British ports, one was sunk. In the following month the British Admiralty finally agreed to organise a convoy system, with the merchant ships gathering at designated harbours. For outward convoys these were Falmouth, Lamlash (on the Isle of Arran), Milford Haven, Plymouth and Queenstown (in the west of Ireland). Convoys for Britain congregated at Dakar, Gibraltar, Hampton Roads and New York. Each port was to send off two convoys every eight days.

Seventeen Cardiff ships had been lost in 1915 and thirty-eight in 1916. In spite of the introduction of a convoy system the worst year of the war was to be 1917, when 124 were sunk. From January to May 1917 forty-two Cardiff vessels were destroyed.

Cardiff ships sunk in June included *Merioneth* (3,004), Jenkins Brothers; *Kallundborg* (1,590), Hain; *Enidwen* (3,594), W. & C.T. Jones; *Cheltonian* (4,426), John Mathias & Sons; *Appledore* (3,843), W.J. Tatem; *Heulwen* (4,032), W. & C.T. Jones; *Ribera* (3,511), Humphries (Cardiff); *Darius* (3,426), W.H. Seager; *St. Andrews* (3,613), Morel; *Dart* (3,207), Hain; *Fornebo* (4,259), Harold de Mattos; *Ruperra* (4,232), John Cory & Sons; *South Wales* (3,668), Gibbs & Co; *Haigh Hall* (4,809), Edward Nicholl. The vessels were carrying cargoes such as coal, sugar, iron ore, wheat, oil and rice. They met their end in the North Atlantic, the Mediterranean, off northern Norway and in the waters around the British Isles.

The cruellest month for Cardiff crews was July 1917:

7 July *Southina* (3,506). Built 1899. Owned by Edwards & Sons. Cardiff to Oran (Coal). Torpedoed, near the coast of Algeria, by submarine U-82. One man was lost.

14 July *Exford* (5,886). Built 1914. Owned by W.J. Tatem. New York to Cherbourg (Steel and oats). Torpedoed by U-48 near the Bay of Biscay. Six men were lost.

15 July *Trelissik* (4,168). Built 1909. Owned by Hain. Boston, Mass. to Bordeaux (Oats). Torpedoed in the Bay of Biscay by UC-72. The master and two gunners were taken prisoner.

20 July *Beatrice*. Owned by Cleeve's Western Valleys Anthracite. Penarth to Honfleur (Coal). Torpedoed off the Lizard.

20 July *Trelyon* (3,099). Built 1898. Owned by Hain. Archangel to London (Timber). Hit a mine near Scarborough, and beached.

21 July *Coniston Water* (3,738). Built 1908. Owned by Reardon Smith. Newport (Monmouthshire) to Archangel (Coal). Torpedoed by U-87 off the Hebrides.

21 July *Paddington* (5,084). Built 1899. Owned by Evan Thomas Radcliffe. Cartagena to UK Torpedoed 250 miles west of Ireland. Twenty-nine died.

21 July *Ramillies* (2,935). Built 1892. Owned by John Cory & Sons. Troon to Huelva (Coal). Detained by U-58 in the Atlantic to the west of Ireland, and sunk by gunfire.

23 July *Ashleigh* (6,985). Owned by W.J. Tatem. Built 1917. Tyne to Port Said (Coal). Torpedoed by U-54 300 miles south-west of Ireland.

24 July *Brumaire* (2,324) Built 1901. Owned by the Plisson Steam Navigation Co. Hartlepool to La Spezia (coal). Torpedoed in the Western Approaches by U-46. Two men were lost.

25 July *Monkstone* (3,097). Built 1909. Owned by Elvidge and Morgan. Tyne to Gibraltar (Coal). Torpedoed 250 miles west of the Scillies by U-82.

26 July *Carmarthen* (4,262). Built 1916. Owned by Jenkins Bros. Genoa to Tees (Ballast) Torpedoed by UC-50 off the Lizard.

26 July *Ludgate* (3,708). Built 1906. Owned by Williams and Mordey. Huelva to Mersey (Iron ore). Hit a mine off the coast of County Cork. Twenty-four men were lost.

27 July *Begona* (2,407). Built 1890. Owned by H. Rees Jones & Co. West Africa to Cork (Phosphates). Torpedoed off the Irish coast.

29 July *Whitehall* (3,158). Built 1905. formerly the *Barnsmore*, the vessel was bought in 1915 by Blow, Richards & Co. Montreal to Ipswich (wheat). Torpedoed and sunk in the Western Approaches. One man lost.

30 July *Ganges* (4,177). Built 1902. Owned by Hain. Barry to La Spezia (Coal). Torpedoed off the coast of Morocco by U-39. One man died.

31 July *Snowdonian* (3,870). Built 1907. Owned by Owen and Watkin Williams. Barry to Freetown (Coal). Detained by U-155 and then sunk with explosive charges, 250 miles south-east of the Azores.

51 The *Canganian* was launched at Glasgow on 14 December 1899 by Mackie and Thomson, and was the third ship to be acquired by Owen and Watkin Williams. During the First World War *Canganian* operated as an Admiralty collier until lost with all hands on 17 November 1916, after hitting a mine.

52 W.J. Tatem's *Torrington* (5,597) at the opening of the Queen Alexandra Dock in 1907, carrying the message 'Cardiff Waifs and Strays. God Bless our King, Queen & Princess'. *Torrington* was a turret-ship, completed by William Doxford & Sons of Sunderland in 1905. On 8 April 1917 the vessel was sunk by a German torpedo 150 miles south-west of the Isles of Scilly.

August was another bad month for Cardiff merchant shipping: *Llandudno* (4,186), Evan Thomas Radcliffe; *Rosemount* (3,044), John Cory & Sons; *Llanishen* (3,837), Evan Thomas Radcliffe; *Blagdon* (1,996), Hansen Brothers; *Maston* (3,881), Thomas and Appleton; *Glocliffe* (2,211), Humphries; *Edernian* (3,588), Owen and Watkin Williams; *Norhilda* (1,175), John Cory & Sons; *Cymrian* (1,014), Owen and Watkin Williams; *Whitecourt* (3,680), Blow, Richards & Co; *Kildonan* (2,118); *Treloske* (3,071), Hain; *Vronwen* (5,714), W. & C.T. Jones; *Grelhame* (3,740), Gould. They were sunk in the Mediterranean, near the Shetland Isles, in the Bay of Biscay and off the coasts of Cornwall, Devon, Suffolk and Yorkshire. Their cargoes included government supplies, timber, herrings, coal, steel, iron ore and sugar.

From January 1918 until the Armistice on 11 November thirty-one more Cardiff vessels were lost.

Between 1914 and 1918 over 200 Cardiff vessels were lost – about 70 per cent of the pre-war fleet. Nearly 15,000 British merchant seamen died during the war.

53 *Starcross* came from the yard of Richardson, Duck & Co. at Stockton-on-Tees, and was built for Anning Brothers in 1894. By 1909 it belonged to W.H. Seager, and was called *Virtus*. Three years later it was sold to Greece, by 1915 was in Norwegian ownership, and was lost when torpedoed on 8 September 1917, on a voyage from New York to Le Havre.

9

RIOT, BOOM, DEPRESSION

In the months after the Armistice, sporadic racial violence erupted in British ports – in February 1919 at South Shields, in May at Liverpool and on Friday 6 June at Newport, where windows of colonial seamen's lodgings were smashed, Chinese laundries were attacked and furniture was taken from two houses and burned. On Saturday night the police had to confront another mob, which was set on storming boarding houses. Four days later a white man was killed in Barry, which led to groups of men roaming about the streets and throwing bricks through windows. Sixty extra policemen, and a downpour, kept things fairly quiet after that.

The flash-point in Cardiff came just after 10.00p.m. on 11 June. In a report to the Home Office the Town Clerk wrote: 'The riots began on the evening of Wednesday June the 11th, when some white women accompanied by men of colour were passing through one of the main streets of Cardiff on their return from a picnic.

Some uncomplimentary references having been made by people in the street, the coloured men left the carriages to attack the people there, and an affray took place in which a number of white men and police were injured and one man was killed'. The man – white, aged twenty – had his throat cut in Caroline Street. Later the same night Arab boarding houses were attacked.

Troops were ordered to readiness but it rained all the next day and nothing happened until the evening, when white people came out to target a boarding house on Adam Street. Tension built up as about 1,000 people mobbed Arab restaurants and boarding houses on Bute Street. From one house shots were fired at the crowd, and one of its residents died of a fractured skull after being hit on the head. Groups went looking for 'coloured' men in Riverside and at Cardiff General railway station, Caroline Street, Millicent Street and Tredegar Street. A man was killed by a shot fired into the crowd from a besieged house.

On Friday 13th some colonial seamen took the opportunity to get out, escorted from the town by constables and shadowed by a menacing crowd. There were some disturbances during the day and by evening thousands of people were milling around at the bottom end of St Mary Street and on Custom House Street, so it was decided to keep them away from the southern part of Butetown by stationing policemen at the bridges and forming a line of constables across Bute Street. Some of the more aggressive rioters tried to break through, but were repulsed by the police, who set about them with truncheons. The windows of a Malay sailors' house were broken and stones hurled at the occupants.

Saturday was quieter, although policemen used their truncheons on some members of a crowd unhappy at the arrest of two men. As a result of three days of mayhem, three men lay dead and many people had been injured, there was a good deal of damage to property and incalculable harm had been done to future race relations. A fortnight later the First World War ended officially when the Treaty of Versailles was signed.

What lay behind the Cardiff riots? There was considerable racial prejudice, as was demonstrated eight years before during the seamen's strike of 1911, and this was exacerbated by other factors. At the start of the war many British seamen joined the armed forces and foreign seamen, especially those from what were now enemy countries, also left British merchant ships. It became increasingly difficult to find crews, pay-rates went up, and more and more colonial seamen were recruited to make up the shortfall. Minority communities expanded in most British ports. The *South Wales Daily News* (2 September 1916) worried about what it called 'these alien classes... Arabs, coloured men and Chinamen have benefited considerably from the changed conditions... today there are more Arabs and coloured men entering Cardiff than ever before'.

Following the Armistice, more and more ex-servicemen returned to a Cardiff where there were problems finding accommodation and very few jobs to be had. In July 1919 70 per cent of those unemployed in Cardiff were former servicemen. Without jobs or proper housing, many looked for someone to blame. The *South Wales News* reported the comments of some of the rioters, including, 'We went out to France, and when we came back we find these foreigners have got our jobs, our businesses and our houses, and we can't get rid of them', and 'I did it for the benefit of the seamen, of whom I am one, and cannot get a job because of these niggers being here. We have tried other ways; we now intend to take the law into our own hands'.

The view of the *Western Mail* was that:

> The Government ought to declare it to be part of the national policy that this country is not to be regarded as an emigration field, that no more immigrants (as distinguished from visitors) can be admitted and that immigrants who have not been assimilated must return whence they came. This must apply to the blackmen from the West Indies as well as the United States. The Arabs are mainly seamen and their repatriation ought to be a simpler matter.

Who were these people that the *Western Mail* wanted to deport? In his report to the Home Office, immediately after the riots, the Chief Constable wrote:

> The coloured men comprised principally West Indians, Somalis, Arabs, and a few Indians. They live in boarding houses kept by coloured masters in an area bounded on the north by Bridge Street, the east by the Taff Vale Railway not very far distant, on the west by the Glamorganshire Canal, and on the south by Patrick Street. Some of the Arabs and Somalis live in the northernmost portion of this area but the majority, particularly the West Indian negroes, live in the southern portion. The area is divided by a junction of the Glamorganshire canal which has two bridges, one in Bute Street and one at East Wharf.

The colonial seamen saw things differently from the rioters and the *Western Mail*: they were not foreigners, but British subjects, who had served during the war, braving storms and attacks by submarines, with many men being killed in the process, to bring food and other essential supplies to the British Isles. The survivors now found themselves unable to get jobs, because white men were preferred, and they wanted equality of treatment. One estimate of the numbers of such seamen unemployed in Cardiff at the time of the riots was: West Indians – 400, Somalis – 200, West Africans – 100, 'Portuguese, Indians, Cingalese and Malays'– 60, Egyptians – 50.

For those tired of hostility and unemployment there was already a repatriation scheme for seamen stranded in Britain, and six hundred had left by August 1919. Men were offered £1 on departure and £5 on arrival at their destination. Money was also given to get items, but not 'luxuries', back from the pawnbroker. Those married to 'non-white' women could leave if they had a guarantee of accommodation; men with white wives were not eligible for the scheme.

Many did not want to leave because Butetown was now home, while others were still in debt to boarding-house masters. The repatriation scheme was not generous and there were difficulties in finding ships. Those who were allocated a vessel found that the voyage might not always be uneventful. The SS *Orca*, owned by the Pacific Steam Navigation Co., sailed from Cardiff for the West Indies in August 1919. The owners later wrote to the government:

The *Orca* left Cardiff on 31 August last after having embarked, in accordance with Government instructions, 225 coloured civilians, mostly Mercantile Marine ratings. The Commander of the *Orca* reports that they came on board with the apparent intention of defying authority, and had in their possession Revolvers and Knives.

The ship called at Le Havre on 12 September, where eighty military prisoners, guarded by sixteen soldiers, were brought to the ship. The *Orca's* captain asked for the escort to be strengthened, and thirty-four more soldiers were embarked.

Had this not been done, the ship might have been in serious danger, as she was not adequately protected against such a number of coloured criminals.

Trouble flared soon after leaving Le Havre, when five men ended up in the cells. Attempts were made to free them, and on 20 September the five prisoners 'made a determined attack upon the crew and a number of coloured soldiers gathered round in a threatening manner, so much so that it was found necessary to open fire, one convict being wounded and a soldier shot dead. There was afterwards a general uprising, which was so serious that the Commander of the *Orca* sent out a wireless call for assistance, but with no result'. At Barbados the Captain of HMS *Yarmouth* 'kindly took the confined prisoners out of the *Orca,* had he not done so, one fears to think what might have been the consequence'.

The midsummer riots in Cardiff had damaged the city's reputation, and set back race relations for many years. As the disturbances petered out, the *South Wales News* gave as its opinion that:

The cowardly attacks upon black men must be rigorously dealt with, for the position of the South Wales ports is such that there must be no suspicion of disadvantage attaching to sailors – whatever the nationality – who have to frequent them… Just now, when by mandate under the Peace Treaty the British Empire's obligation to the dark races is being extended, it is all the more necessary to insist upon fair play and equal treatment to everyman, whatever his colour.

Twenty-eight men were brought to court, of whom eighteen were white, and received penalties ranging from fines up to imprisonment with hard labour. At the Assizes ten white men were found guilty of 'riotous assembly' and sent to prison, the longest sentence being twenty months. Five Arabs were charged with firing guns – three were freed because their lives were being threatened, one was sentenced to three months' hard labour (he shot at a policeman who came into his house when there was a mob outside) and another, who also fired at a policeman, to fifteen months.

The Post-War Shipping Boom

The number of Cardiff ship-owning firms doubled in 1919, and their fleet expanded to around 300 ships. A similar phenomenon could be observed in other British ports, but it was particularly evident at Cardiff – in August 1919 alone, seventeen new companies were hoping to attract investment of about £2,000,000. In the first three months of 1920, twenty-nine companies were looking to raise £6,000,000.

Many people took it for granted that there would be a surge in the post-war demand for vessels and concluded that shipping ownership was a good way to make money. The wartime governmental controls on the use of ships were in the process of being removed and would be gone by October 1919. Financial institutions were also optimistic about the prospects for making money, and banks were lending up to 80 per cent of the purchase price of a vessel. Shipping company managers were not put off by the prospect of large mortgage repayments, since their own remuneration was based not on the profitability of the ship, but on its gross earnings. Freight rates were rising, encouraging investors' optimism.

This stampede to set up new shipping companies led to a 30 per cent rise in the cost of a new vessel in one year. There was a parallel rush to buy second-hand, and many antiquated steamers were snapped up at inflated prices.

For a while, all went well, and big profits were made, with dividends of the order of 13 per cent to 25 per cent being paid to investors. A rosy view of the industry's prospects seemed justified, but some of the more established owners were wary, and got rid of their vessels for the inflated sums then being offered.

The crash came in May 1920, when freight rates began an accelerating slide, dropping by 75 per cent in a few months and, apart from a brief recovery around 1926/27, staying at that sort of level until the Second World War. The rates dropped because there was not, in reality, a shortage of shipping – although vessels had been lost in the war any shortfall had been more than made up by the construction of new vessels, particularly through the emergency shipbuilding programmes of the United States, and in 1919 about 2,000 new vessels came off the world's slipways. There was now more tonnage available than before the war, so with more cargo space available than cargo to fill it, freight rates were bound to fall.

Another major problem for Cardiff was its dependence on the export of coal and related products, which accounted for 90 per cent of the Bute Docks' export trade, making the port and its shipping very exposed to fluctuations in output from the collieries. In April 1925 Britain returned to the Gold Standard, which revalued the pound sterling and made British exports, including coal, more expensive. Markets had been lost because of the effects of the war, with the South American trade coming to be dominated by the United States, and coal from Germany supplied as war reparations diminishing the demand for British coal in France and Italy. There was a worldwide decline in the demand for coal because steam-engines providing power for factories were being superseded by the internal combustion engine, and oil began to take over from coal to power ships' boilers. Production of coal in Wales was also affected by industrial disputes, in particular the stoppages of April to June 1921 and May to November 1926. Between 1920 and 1937 more than 240 collieries closed in south Wales, with the number of people employed going from 270,000 to about 130,000.

With less coal to be transported and a surfeit of vessels competing for cargoes, Cardiff shipping firms were in trouble, with earnings lower and many vessels not needed. Companies could no longer afford the high running costs (particularly of the older ships), not to mention the mortgage interest payments. The value of the ships themselves plummeted, often fetching – if they could be sold at all – only 20 per cent of their original purchase price. It became inevitable that ships would be taken out of service, and by October 1922 nearly 19,000 tons of shipping were laid up at Cardiff. (In Britain the total was about 824,000 tons). Cardiff firms which were wound up included: Anglo-Belgique (started in 1916, finished in 1929), Anglo-Celtic (1920–35), Aster (1919–32), Berg (1916–24), Bride (1907–23), Bristol Channel Steamers (1919–32)), British Dominions (1919–29), Care and Marquand (1919–32), County (1918–24), Dean (1919–25), J.C. & W.T. Gould (1920–25), Hansen (1916–24), Hinde (1915–32), Instone (1915–24), James, Muers and Griffin (1915–21), Leeston (1916–31), Llewellyn (1919–29), Loyal Line (1919–32), Lyndon (1919–24), Marine Transport (1919–23), Morgan and Cadogan (1915–26), Penmark (1919–31), Sovereign (1916–26), Thompson (1919–24).

Cardiff Docks 1918–39

In the immediate post-war period, most British ports – including Cardiff – were unable to cope with the volume of traffic. Vessels could queue sometimes for days, possibly for weeks, to discharge or load their cargoes, and goods accumulated on wharves or in warehouses. Cardiff coal trimmers were working fewer hours and a vessel might now take nearly four times as long to load. Industrial disputes were likely to disrupt the flow of cargoes to the port. Delays in loading led to log-jams of railway wagons and hundreds sat in sidings at the port, out of action, but needed urgently back at the colliery.

The docks and railways of south Wales were amalgamated by the *Grouping of Railways Act 1921* into the Great Western Railway Group, with the GWR Chief Docks Manager installed at Cardiff. Measured by 'tonnage handled', Cardiff was now the third largest British port, with nearly seven miles of quays, at four main docks. The north side of the Queen Alexandra Dock was devoted to food imports from Australia, Canada, New Zealand, Spain and the Middle East. The south side dealt with the coal exports, and near at hand was the patent fuel factory. Iron ore for the Dowlais Works was discharged at Roath Dock, from which steel rails and sleepers were exported. The Bute Docks were licensed to import live animals, and there was a cattle lair and an auction ring. Other facilities included Spillers and Bakers flour mills and grain silos, and the fish quay and ice factory of Neale and West.

The coal owners' response to the return to the Gold Standard in April 1925, and to the general decline in the market for coal, was to demand that the miners must work longer hours for 10 to 25 per cent less pay. This was of course rejected, the miners were locked out by the employers and almost 2 million workers stopped work in sympathy. This general strike lasted from 4 to 12 May 1926, but the miners did not go back until November. In Cardiff, the men at the Dowlais Works came out, as did the transport workers (one result was that, on the first day, there were 3,345 railway wagons stuck in the Cardiff yards) but the seamen refused to strike. Some city trams were kept going by volunteers, who were often assaulted for their efforts, and crowds had to be broken up by the police. Over 600 'special constables' were enrolled, some of whom patrolled the railway lines.

The government sent troops to key installations throughout the country and warships appeared at the main ports: Cardiff received a battalion of infantry, a submarine and a cruiser. In the docks volunteers managed to operate some tugs and a grain elevator and, escorted by the Royal Navy, unloaded potatoes, fish and cattle.

The Trades Union Congress called off the strike on 12 May, and five days later the dock workers returned, followed by the tugboat men on the 25th. For the first time, the Great Western Railway had to import coal for its locomotives, and between 14 June and 31 December over 100 cargoes were discharged at Barry, Cardiff and Penarth (plus twenty-eight for the London Midland and Scottish Railway).

During the late 1920s there were a few calls by ocean liners, as attempts were made to drum up a passenger trade through Cardiff. Given the nature of the port – grubby, with coal dust everywhere, and no facilities for passengers – it was unlikely that these could succeed. On 29 July 1928 the United States Lines *George Washington* brought members of the Loyal Order of Moose to a convention at Cardiff. Not long afterwards, Cunard's *Scythia,* on passage from New York to Liverpool, left her usual route to anchor in the Roads. Welsh-Americans on their way to the Royal National Eisteddfod held at Treorchy from 6 to 11 August 1928 were ferried ashore by Campbell's steamer, and continued their journey by special train from Bute Road station. Their efforts were rewarded when the Scranton Male Choir from Pennsylvania was awarded first prize at the eisteddfod, with Cwmbach, from the Cynon Valley, as runners-up.

In the previous century ships carrying cargoes of iron had sometimes taken emigrants as well, and during the 1850s many people went from Cardiff to the United States and to Australia on vessels such as the *St Peter, Kathorn, Kate Sutherland*, and *Bothnia*. In May 1851, Batchelor Brothers had launched the *Taff* specifically for carrying migrants, and a month later it left for New York. The South Wales Atlantic Steamship Company had inaugurated a passenger service to New York in 1872 , but it was not a success. Now, in the late 1920s, the owners of the Bute Docks (the Great Western Railway) decided that it was time to try again and made a determined effort to encourage people to sail from Cardiff. The *Canadian Railway and Marine World* informed its readers that

Canadian Pacific Steamships Ltd, on April 6 (1929), added Cardiff, on the Bristol Channel, as a port of call for outgoing passengers, the first ship to call being the *Montrose*, which

54 The passenger liner *George Washington* arrived in Penarth Roads on 29 July 1928, bringing American members of the Loyal Order of Moose to their convention at Cardiff.

left Liverpool on April 5th. During the St Lawrence navigation season, several calls will be made at Cardiff. There is a good deal of emigration from South Wales to Canada and the use of Cardiff as a port of embarkation will be a convenience to the emigrants as well as to passengers from the English midland counties.

The *Western Mail* reported that 'The CPR authorities are delighted with the facilities that Cardiff offers as a passenger port, and are enthusiastic for the future of the trade which is being inaugurated today'. On Saturday 6 April 1929 P&A Campbell carried trippers down Channel to meet the *Montrose*, and those emigrants who had boarded at Liverpool were greeted by the singing of Welsh hymns from the paddle steamer. The responses from those on the liner included – according to the *Western Mail*'s reporter – a cry of 'Play up Cardiff City!' A special train from Paddington brought the migrants who were to embark at the Queen Alexandra Dock, including a party of 'young Empire settlers who have undergone a course of training in farm work under the Government scheme'. *Montrose* arrived in the late afternoon. A dinner was given on board for the Lord Mayor and other 'civic dignitaries', while the CPR showed the film *The Birth of a Liner* at the Cory Hall 'with the object of creating public interest in transatlantic travel'. The *Montrose* left in the early hours of Sunday morning.

Monday's local paper – under the headline CARDIFF A SECOND LIVERPOOL – saw the liner's visit as 'an event of considerable moment in the history of the port,' and carried an advertisement for a call which was to be made three weeks later by Cunard's *Alaunia*, to pick up passengers for Quebec and Montreal. Two calls were made

55 During 1929 an attempt was made to develop Cardiff as an embarkation port for migrants to Canada. The first vessel to call, on 6 April, was Canadian Pacific's *Montrose*.

by passenger liners in the next month, and then no more until March and April of the following year, when there were four. The GWR's attempts to drum up a transatlantic passenger trade ended with the visit by White Star's *Baltic* in August 1930.

The Cardiff Fleet in the Mid-1930s

Between 1921 and 1931 nearly a quarter of a million people moved away from south Wales. In August 1931 police in Cardiff used their truncheons to break up a demonstration by the unemployed, and in the summer of 1936 mass protests took place throughout south Wales. The quantity of coal exported through Cardiff had halved (compared with 1913) and at Penarth had dropped by 75 per cent. On 6 July 1936 Penarth Dock was closed, except for access to the ship-repairing facilities, the last vessel to leave being the *Amiens* taking coal to Rochefort.

In spite of such economic and social conditions, some owners began to buy vessels again in the mid-1930s, encouraged by the government's tramp shipping subsidy introduced in 1935. Some of the new ships acquired were motor vessels, which needed a smaller crew (there were no firemen) and were much easier to bunker than their coal-fired predecessors. But shipping freight rates were low and in 1935 around 60 per cent of Cardiff vessels were laid up, and there were only half as many ship-owning firms and half as many vessels as in the last years before the First World War. Some of the companies still in existence were:

Greyhound Motors Ltd. & P. & A. Campbell Ltd.

SAILINGS from HOTWELLS (Bristol)
(Weather and circumstances permitting) on

Good Friday, April 19th

Association Football Match at Cardiff: **CARDIFF CITY v. BRISTOL ROVERS.**

CLEVEDON, CARDIFF, PENARTH, LYNMOUTH, and ILFRACOMBE

Leave Bristol 9.0 a.m. Leave Ilfracombe 4.0 p.m., Lynmouth 4.30, Penarth 6.15, Cardiff 4.30 or 6.40, Clevedon 5.30 or 7.30.

RETURN FARES—CLEVEDON 2/-, CARDIFF or PENARTH 4/-, LYNMOUTH or ILFRACOMBE 7/6.

In connection with this Trip, Greyhound Motors Ltd. will run Buses from various parts of the City to Hotwells Landing Stage (alongside of Steamer) as under :—

ROUTE No. 1.	Depart.	Fare		ROUTE No. 3.	Depart.	Fare		ROUTE No. 5.	Depart.	Fare
Eastville Park Gates	8.20 a.m.	9d.		Brislington Tram Depot	8.25 a.m.	8d.		Eastville Trams (White Swan)	8.25 a.m.	8d.
Ashley Hill Station (Footpath)	8.24 a.m.	9d.		Three Lamps	8.31 a.m.	6d.		Warwick Road	8.28 a.m.	7d.
Junct. Muller and Glo'ster Road	8.29 a.m.	7d.		Bath Bridge	8.33 a.m.	6d.		St. Nicholas Road	8.31 a.m.	7d.
Nevil Road	8.31 a.m.	7d.		Bristol Bridge	8.35 a.m.	4d.		Horsefair	8.34 a.m.	5d.
Zetland Road	8.33 a.m.	6d.		Tram Centre (Opp. Hippo.)	8.38 a.m.	3d.		Park Row (Top of Park Street)	8.38 a.m.	3d.
Cheltenham Road (Arley Chapel)	8.35 a.m.	6d.		Jacob's Wells (Hotwell Road)	8.42 a.m.	3d.		Jacob's Wells (Hotwell Road)	8.41 a.m.	3d.
Jamaica Street (King Square Ave.)	8.37 a.m.	6d.								
Park Row (Top of Park Street)	8.39 a.m.	3d.		ROUTE No. 4.						
Jacob's Wells (Hotwell Road)	8.42 a.m.	3d.		Lawrence Hill Station	8.25 a.m.	8d.		ROUTE No. 6.		
ROUTE No. 2.				Barrow Road	8.27 a.m.	8d.		Bushy Park	8.30 a.m.	8d.
Westbury Car Terminus	8.25 a.m.	9d.		West Street (Trinity Church)	8.29 a.m.	8d.		St. John's Lane (Park Ave.)	8.33 a.m.	7d.
White Tree	8.30 a.m.	8d.		Old Market (Carey's Lane)	8.32 a.m.	6d.		Bedminster Tram Depot	8.36 a.m.	6d.
Blackboy (Trams)	8.33 a.m.	6d.		Horsefair	8.36 a.m.	5d.		North St. (" Hen & Chicken ")	8.39 a.m.	3d.
Whiteladies Rd. (Clifton D. Stn.)	8.37 a.m.	6d.		Tram Centre (Opp. Hippo.)	8.39 a.m.	3d.		Frayne Road	8.41 a.m.	3d.
Triangle (Opp. Picture House)	8.40 a.m.	3d.		Jacob's Wells (Hotwell Road)	8.42 a.m.	3d.		Ashton Swing Bridge	8.43 a.m.	3d.
Jacob's Wells (Hotwell Road)	8.43 a.m.	3d.								

Evening CRUISE UP RIVER SEVERN (passing Aust and towards Sheperdine). Leave Bristol 6.50 p.m., back about 9.30 p.m. Fare **2/-**.

Single Trip to CLEVEDON, PENARTH, and CARDIFF. Leave Bristol 9.45 p.m.

☞ NO CIRCULAR TRIP BOOKINGS THIS DAY. ☜

For further particulars apply to P. & A. CAMPBELL Ltd., 1 Britannia Buildings, Cumberland Basin.

Y. & W. GOULDING, NELSON STREET, BRISTOL.—1/1935. (2M.)

56 A P&A Campbell poster, 1935.

The Hain Steamship Company. The firm's roots were in the Cornish town of St Ives, but it had been closely connected with Cardiff since 1881. Sixteen vessels had been lost in the war, following which the company was bought by P&O, although its vessels were still controlled from the Cardiff office. In 1923 the Roath Engineering Company was formed, to provide a repair facility for the Hain fleet.

The Hain ship *Trevessa* was lost on 4 June 1923 in the Indian Ocean. The vessel began life as the *Imkenturm* (5,004), built at Flensburg in 1909 for the Hansa Line of Bremen. Laid up during the First World War at Surabaya, at the end of hostilities *Imkenturm* was taken over by the Shipping Controller as part of the reparations programme, and acquired by Hain in 1920. *Trevessa* left Liverpool on 2 January 1923 and had arrived in the Indian Ocean via Canada, the Panama Canal and then Auckland, Wellington, Lyttleton, Timaru, Dunedin, Melbourne and Sydney, Port Pirie and Fremantle. She was now on the way to Durban, and then Antwerp, with a cargo of zinc concentrates. In the early hours of 4 June, with the weather deteriorating, the vessel began to take in water, forcing the crew to abandon ship. The steamer *Runic* searched for survivors after hearing an SOS message, but found no one. *Trevessa*'s crew were in two lifeboats, twenty men in Captain Cecil Foster's boat and twenty-four in that commanded by First Officer James C. Stewart Smith. Both boats were about 8m long x 2.5m broad x 1m deep, equipped

57 The Hain Steamship Company's *Trevessa* foundered in the Indian Ocean on 4 June 1923. The forty-four men took to two lifeboats. Captain Foster's boat reached land after a voyage of over 1,500 miles and twenty-three days, but three men had died. First Officer Stewart Smith's took twenty-five days to sail to Mauritius, having sailed 1,750 miles; seven men died, one after being brought ashore.

with a mast and sail, eight pulling oars and a steering oar. It was decided to make for Mauritius, about 1,700 miles away. The boats tried to stay together but this proved to be impossible. The Captain noted in his log on the sixth day (9 June) '8 a.m. Wished each other the best of luck – gave three cheers and we shook the reef out, hoisted sail and carried on. Moderate W.S.W. breeze, steering about N.N.W. true, issued milk and biscuit ration'. The water ration, issued at 2.00p.m. daily, was one third of a cigarette tin each (about three tablespoons). By the fifteenth day the log noted, 'All hands pretty well battered. Lips cracked previously, but we have healed up since we had the heavy rain. Mouths still horrible with white slime'. The Captain's boat reached land after twenty-three days, arriving at Rodriguez Island on the evening of 26 June. Three men had died during the voyage of over 1,550 miles and the survivors were all 'weak and emaciated'. The First Officer's boat managed to reach Mauritius after a journey of twenty-five days and nearly 1,750 miles. Seven men died on the way, one after reaching land.

As the Union Castle liner *Goorkha*, carrying some of the survivors, made her way up the Thames, 'all the vessels were dressed with flags and blowing their syrens'. At the end of the inquiry into the loss of the *Trevessa*: 'The Court is unable to find words adequately to express its members' admiration of the fine seamanship and resolution of the officers, the splendid discipline and courage of the crew, both European and non-European. The Court desires to express deep sympathy with the relatives of those who lost their lives'.

Sir William Reardon Smith (he was made a baronet in 1920) operated thirty-five ships, 80 per cent of them under ten years old. As well as the traditional Cardiff tramping trade, there was also a liner service from 1928 to 1937 carrying freight from the west coast of America to the United Kingdom. In 1936 the firm was able to take advantage of the provisions of the *British Shipping (Assistance) Act*, which aimed to try to get rid of surplus tonnage and encourage the building of new vessels, thus providing work for British shipyards. The 'scrap and build' programme made low-interest finance available, on condition that for every ton built two tons were scrapped. Using this scheme the Reardon Smith company was able to buy the new motor vessels *Bradford City* (4,952) and *Cornish City* (4,952).

Neale and West owned seventeen trawlers, one of which, *Miura*, was lost on the night of 29 March 1927, wrecked on the coast of north Cornwall near Morwenstow. Five men were saved, but seven died. *Nodzu* was sold in 1929 to Cam and Sons, of Sydney, Australia. Built in 1920 by Cook, Welton and Gemmell of Beverley, the vessel was renamed *Olive Cam*, and chartered in 1935 for minesweeping trials with the Royal Australian Navy. During the Second World War, as HMAS *Olive Cam*, she served as a minesweeper, but was to be lost after going aground in 1954.

During the twenties and thirties Neale and West bought a number of new vessels: 1927 – *Hatsuse*, *Kunishi* and *Suma*; 1928 – *Honjo* and *Sasebo*; 1929 – *Asama*, *Nodzu*, *Oku* and *Yashima*; 1931 – *Muroto*, *Naniwa*, *Oyama* and *Sata*; 1939 – *Akita*.

Evan Thomas Radcliffe lost twenty of their twenty-eight ships during the war. By the mid-1930's the company owned sixteen vessels, eleven of which were laid up during 1933.

W.J. Tatem. At the end of the First World War, W.J. Tatem (by now Lord Glanely) sold off his remaining eight ships, replacing them gradually: one in 1919, two in 1920 (one of which – *Pilton* – ran aground on Sully beach, near Penarth, in December 1924 and was stuck there for three months), three in 1925, four in 1927, two in 1928 and two in 1930. From 1933 to 1938 Tatem sold seven ships, buying *Northleigh* (5,450) in 1937 and *Chulmleigh* (5,455), *Goodleigh* (5,448), and *Lady Glanely* (5,497) in 1938. Shipping was not the millionaire Tatem's only interest. He had become famous as a race-horse owner – known to the Turf fraternity as 'Old Guts and Gaiters' – winning the Derby in 1919 with *Grand Parade*, the Oaks in 1930 (*Rose of England*), the St Leger (1930 *Singapore*; 1937 *Chulmleigh*), the 2,000 Guineas in 1934 (*Colombo*) and the 1,000 Guineas with *Dancing Time* in 1941.

John Cory & Sons. Between 1914 and 1918 the firm lost twenty ships by enemy action, but one Cory vessel managed to sink a submarine. The *Ross* (2,666) was travelling from Seville to the Clyde with a cargo of iron ore when a German submarine came to the surface close by, only to be rammed and sunk by the *Ross*. On 22 April 1916 the *Ross* was in its turn lost – torpedoed in the Bay of Biscay. The crew took to their boats and ended up in Le Havre. During the war Cory's bought the Orders and Handford Shipping Company of Newport, with its seven ships. In 1918 the Cory company had nine ships, reduced to three by 1936.

Hale (Derwen Shipping) ran eight vessels in the traditional Cardiff trade of coal out and grain home. Their fleet was sold off in 1931/32, seven ships going to Greece and one – *Grelhead* (4,274) built in 1915 – being bought by Walter T. Gould.

OGDEN'S CIGARETTES.

LORD GLANELY.

58 Lord Glanely (W.J. Tatem) – millionaire owner of ships and race-horses – from a series of cigarette cards of 'Turf Personalities'.

Chellew. Six vessels were lost in the First World War, and in 1918 the single-ship companies were abandoned, with the remaining eight ships being placed in the new 'R.B. Chellew Steam Navigation Company'. The main office of the company moved from Truro to Cardiff in 1920. R.B. Chellew died in 1929 and the firm was sold in the following year to F.C. Perman of London.

B&S Shipping. Two separate ship-owning companies formed in November 1926 – the Barry Shipping Company and the St Quentin Shipping Company – came together in 1933 under the management umbrella of 'B&S Shipping'. The firm was able to buy four new vessels through the 'scrap and build' scheme: in 1936 *St Helena* (4,313), *St Margaret* (4,312) and *St Clears* (4,312) and in 1937 *St Rosario* (4,312). The vessels tramped, but gradually came to concentrate on carrying coal to Argentina with return cargoes of grain. From 1937 B&S ships were employed on a liner service to South America. In March 1939 the name 'Barry Shipping Co' was replaced by 'South American Saint Line'.

59 This ship was built at West Hartlepool in 1915, as *Nolisement*, for Morel Ltd. It was sold in 1928 to W.H. Seager, who gave it the name *Darius*, before selling to Greek owners in 1933. The vessel, by then called *Balboa*, was broken up at Savona in 1959.

W.H. Seager & Co. At the end of the war Seager's owned four ships. William Seager's second son had been killed at the battle of Neuve Chapelle while serving with the 10th South Wales Borderers, and as a memorial his parents built the Willie Seager Memorial Homes on Newport Road, Cardiff. From 1918 to 1922 the now Sir William Seager was MP for Cardiff East. By 1933 the firm was running five vessels: *Amicus*, *Beatus*, *Campus*, *Fiscus* and *Salvus*, which voyaged to the Mediterranean, the River Plate, Australia and New Zealand.

Claymore Shipping Co. The coal exporter Charles Clay started the company in 1919, buying four vessels in 1920. By 1936 there were two.

Frederick Jones lost no vessels in the war. At the end of the post-war boom the company owned four vessels, but by 1921 they were all laid up on the Torridge and ten years later were idle again. In 1934/35 all four were laid up at the East Bute Dock, only to be rescued by the Soviet Union – *Margam Abbey*, *Neath Abbey* and *Singleton Abbey* left Cardiff together, being taken on time charter to Archangel. The other Jones ship – *Tintern Abbey* – was also sent off to Archangel for timber, so that the whole fleet was in the Russian port at the same time.

Owen & Watkin Williams. By the early '20s the firm owned two ships, but then – in 1923 – acquired one of the first motor vessels to be bought by a Cardiff owner, the new *Margretian* (2,577), which appears to be the first motor vessel built by Charles Hill & Sons of Bristol. The ship was to be employed on the Williams's 'Golden Cross Line' Mediterranean routes. Two years later came a motor vessel intended for tramping, *Silurian* (6,903), constructed on the Clyde. These vessels were expensive to buy, the

60 *Daybreak* was built in 1925 by R. Thompson & Sons, Sunderland, for the Claymore Shipping Company. It was sold to Greek owners in 1934 and was sunk on 8 October 1942 by a German submarine in the Indian Ocean, with the loss of five men.

engines turned out to be unreliable, and freight rates were low. By June 1925 the four Williams vessels were all laid up. On 2 March 1928 the *Western Mail* informed its readers that the *Silurian* – 'Cardiff's largest motor vessel' – had been sold to Furness Withy & Co. for between £70,000 and £80,000. (It had been offered for sale by auction in the previous December, but withdrawn at £66,000.) The last vessel owned by the firm, *Margretian*, was sold four years later.

The Spanish Civil War

The Spanish civil war started on 18 July 1936 with a rebellion against the government of the Spanish Republic. The war struck a further blow to the Cardiff shipping industry, disrupting the imports of Spanish iron ore and the export of steam coal, but profits could still be made by owners willing to charter their vessels to the Spanish government. High rates were paid and crews received a bonus for each voyage – seen as compensation for the possibility of being shot at or bombed. The Frederick Jones steamer *Neath Abbey* took a cargo from Rotterdam to Alicante, discharging on 8 April 1937, and made a profit on this one voyage equal to a year's normal earnings.

By April 1937 the insurgent Franco forces were blockading the northern Spanish ports, and the British Board of Trade announced that it was not safe for ships to go there. On 8 April the Admiralty in London ordered those British ships en route to Bilbao to divert to St Jean de Luz, where they should wait for further orders. On the next day, among the vessels at St Jean de Luz were *Sarastone* of Swansea (Captain Jones) and two

Cardiff ships, *Macgregor* (Captain Jones) and *Marie Llewellyn* (Captain Jones). A journalist with an eye for a story invented the nicknames, allegedly referring to their cargoes, of 'Potato' Jones, 'Ham and Egg' Jones and 'Corn Cob Jones'.

On 11 April the *Seven Seas Spray* (Captain Roberts) arrived from Alicante with a cargo including tinned food, olive oil, salt and wine. Owned by Alfred S. Pope of Mount Stuart Square, Cardiff, the *Seven Seas Spray* had been built at Ardrossan in 1919, and had acquired her present name only recently – she was formerly the *Glassford*, and the *Baron Elibank*. Her claim to fame was as the vessel that rammed the Nantucket lightship (on 20 December 1935), putting it out of action. On 15 April the *Sarastone* was ordered to Bayonne and, as she left, was followed by 'Potato' Jones in *Macgregor*, who set course for Spain. He was back next day, having been warned off by a British destroyer, and departed on the 17th, making for Gibraltar.

The Basque authorities, desperately anxious to get food to Bilbao, offered cash bonuses to the masters of vessels which broke the blockade. On 19 April the *Seven Seas Spray* slipped out of St Jean de Luz. With Captain Roberts on board was his nineteen-year-old daughter Florence, who had been a pupil at Penarth County School for Girls. Disregarding a warning from a British destroyer, he arrived at Bilbao to a hero's welcome on 20 April 1937. Bilbao fell to Franco's forces two months later. Six Cardiff vessels were captured in attempting to embark refugees: at Santander *Kenfig Poole* and *Seabank* (Alfred Pope), *Molton* (Tatem); at Gijon *Candleston Castle* (Branch) and *Yorkbrook* (Angel). They were released after a month or two. The hero of Bilbao, *Seven Seas Spray*, was seized at Santona on 25 August 1937 and not set free until November.

On 6 June 1938 *St Winifred* (B&S Shipping) was bombed in port at Alicante. Five men were killed and the vessel was badly damaged, but was able to be towed to Marseilles, where it was sold. *Yorkbrook* was sunk by bombing at Barcelona, but was raised in January 1940, becoming a Spanish vessel. *Miocene* (Angel) also ended up on the Spanish register after being bombed and sunk at Barcelona (there were no casualties) while discharging benzene.

10

THE SECOND WORLD WAR

At the beginning of the Second World War there were about 170 vessels based at Cardiff. Half of these ships were owned by five companies: the Hain Steamship Co. and Sir William Reardon Smith & Sons owned twenty-four each, with more on order. The next largest firm was Evan Thomas and Radcliffe (fifteen vessels), followed by W.J. Tatem and Constants (South Wales), who operated eleven each. The ships were mostly of the order of 5,000 to 6,200 gross registered tons, and ranged in age from those constructed before the First World War up to those newly built. The seamen had to man such vessels for an extra 'War Risk Payment' of £10 a month – but only £5 for those aged under eighteen.

On 1 September 1939 Germany attacked Poland, whose independence had been guaranteed by Britain and France. As a consequence, Britain declared war on Germany on 3 September. The Ministry of War Transport was given responsibility for directing seaborne trade and the ports and a Port Controller was appointed to run Cardiff and Penarth Docks, assisted by an Emergency Committee made up of people from government departments, local dock managers, and representatives of the armed forces. A prime German war aim was, as in 1914–18, to blockade the United Kingdom, in order to sap the country's ability and will to carry on the war. This was to be done by destroying ships and their cargoes – with mines, and attacks by aircraft, surface raiders and submarines. Docks and their installations were to be put out of action and by 1939 the Luftwaffe had dossiers, with maps and photographs, on all its potential targets in Britain. The information was brought up to date by more reconnaissance flights in the summer of 1940. To meet the threat, Cardiff Docks were put into a state of defence as torpedo 'nets' were installed to protect the dock gates and barrage-balloon sites appeared around the city and the dock area. This 'balloon barrage' was intended to force enemy aircraft to fly higher, where they might make easier targets for anti-aircraft guns, searchlights and fighter aeroplanes. Fake targets were established, including one to the east of Wenvoe, a second near Lavernock and another on the other side of the city near to Peterstone Wentloog. Such decoys tried to simulate the kind of 'lights' that might be seen from the air – the glow from a railway engine's firebox or from an industrial furnace, or the electrical sparks made by a city's tramcars. Fires were lit, to make the German aircrews think that this was their real target, burning from earlier bombing.

61 A German reconnaissance photograph of Cardiff, taken just before the Second World War. The Dowlais Steelworks is in the centre.

The work of the port came to be disrupted by enemy mines laid in the Bristol Channel and the docks could be closed for some days while 'mine-sweeping' took place. Then there were the air raids, aimed not only at the docks, but also at the railways, Dowlais steelworks and the Royal Ordnance factory. On 20 June 1940 the Newcastle steamer *Stesso* (2,290) was damaged and, later, six men were killed when the tanker *San Felipe* (5,919) was hit. During the rest of the year raids continued – often by aircraft appearing singly or in pairs – and on 3 September eleven people were killed at Roath.

The worst raid on Cardiff came on the night of 2 January 1941. The bombers arrived at 6.40p.m. and by the time the 'All Clear' sounded at 4.50 the next morning 165 people were dead, nearly a hundred houses had been completely destroyed and many more badly damaged. Two months later, on 3 March 1941, fifty-one people were killed when incendiary bombs set off conflagrations in several parts of the city. The last bombs fell on Cardiff on 18 May 1943, when forty-one people died. Apart from the considerable damage to property, German air raids on Cardiff – from June 1940 to May 1943 – killed 350 people and seriously injured 500.

From 1942 American military supplies began to pour through Cardiff Docks. To help cope with the new tasks, extra cranes were brought into service, including a 30-ton American floating crane, and a labour force of British and US servicemen was drafted in. Cardiff's ship-repairing facilities were kept busy throughout the war, and Penarth Docks became one of several bases for US Naval units maintaining the landing craft (about 2,500 of them) of the 11th Amphibious Force, destined for Normandy. The dock also accommodated the *Alberte Le Borgne* (3,921) which arrived in 1943. This thirty-year-old vessel, formerly owned by the Compagnie Charles Le Borgne, had been managed by P. Henderson & Co. (on behalf of the government) since 1940, and was a veteran of Atlantic convoys. She was to remain berthed at Penarth, and used to train military personnel in dock operations, in preparation for the Allied invasion. The *Alberte Le Borgne* was broken up in 1947.

'Liberty ships' became a familiar sight, especially during the build-up of military stores and personnel for the invasion of Normandy, as Cardiff was one of the embarkation ports for this vast and complex operation, with men and equipment in temporary transit camps all over south Wales. Liberty ships – based on a British design – were constructed in eighteen new shipyards set up in the United States. Built with components made all over the US, these standard vessels had five holds which could carry over 400 tanks, 2,800 jeeps or 230 million rounds of ammunition.

The first Liberty ship, launched on 21 September 1941, took 150 days to build; 2,750 more vessels were to follow and by 1944 the average time from keel-laying to launch was down to forty-two days. It could be done more quickly, and in 1942 a competition was held to discover which yard could build a Liberty ship in the shortest time. The winner was the Kaiser Yard at Richmond, California, which took four days, fifteen hours and thirty minutes to produce the *Robert E. Peary*. After service in the Pacific and Atlantic, the ship sailed from Cardiff in June 1944, taking men to Omaha Beach. For the next three months the *Robert E. Peary* made regular voyages to France in support of the allied campaign.

62 Soldiers going on board ship. During the war Cardiff handled not only coal and military stores, but embarked and disembarked thousands of military personnel.

Paddle steamers

The Campbell paddle steamers were requisitioned in 1939 at the start of the war, except for the oldest – *Ravenswood* – which was employed from 1941 as an anti-aircraft vessel at Belfast until, two years later, she was renamed HMS *Ringtail* and moved to Liverpool. By 1944 the vessel was being used to carry local military traffic along the south coast of Devon. The rest of the Campbell fleet became minesweepers, manned by men of the naval reserve: *Brighton Queen*, *Britannia* (now HMS *Skiddaw*), *Cambria* (now HMS *Plinlimmon*), *Devonia* and *Westward Ho* were allocated to the Firth of Forth, while *Brighton Belle*, *Glen Avon*, *Glen Gower* (HMS *Glenmore* from 1941), *Glen Usk* and *Waverley* (HMS *Snaefell*) were stationed at North Shields.

Eight of the paddle steamers were involved in 'Operation Dynamo', the evacuation of 330,000 British and French soldiers from Dunkirk and adjoining beaches, from 26 May to 4 June 1940. All the vessels came under attack from the air and by artillery near the coast. The *Brighton Belle* was lost on 28 May, after hitting the underwater wreck of a recently sunk vessel off Ramsgate, although all the troops and crew were saved. On 1 June the *Brighton Queen* (originally the Barry Railway Company's *Gwalia*) was making her way back to Britain, carrying over 700 men, when she was bombed and sank within minutes with great loss of life. *Devonia*, damaged by bombs and shells, was beached in order to be used as a jetty for embarking soldiers. *Glen Avon* was hit by shellfire, which killed five and injured others, but managed to bring back a total of 900 men. *Snaefell*'s overall tally of men saved was nearly 1,000, but the vessel was to be lost a year later, sunk by bombs off the north-east coast of England. *Glen Gower* brought back 1,200 and *Plinlimmon* around 900. *Westward Ho*, although damaged and with six men dead, managed to transport 1,600.

Late in 1941 the six paddle steamers began to operate barrage balloons and in 1942 left their minesweeping duties to become anti-aircraft vessels, escorting coastal convoys. The steamers were deployed (not all together) at various times on the Thames, at Harwich, the Firth of Forth and off the Isle of Wight. The *Glen Avon* was lost in September 1944 when the vessel began to break up in a gale off the coast of Normandy and had to be abandoned; forty-six people were rescued, but fifteen died. *Glenmore* and *Skiddaw* were sent to support the balloon barrage protecting Antwerp, with *Glen Usk* in a similar role.

By 1945 the Campbell fleet – eleven in 1939 – had been reduced to four. In June 1947 the *Empress Queen* arrived. On order at the start of the war, she had been launched at Troon in February 1940, requisitioned as an anti-aircraft vessel and sent to the Thames under the name *Queen Eagle*. In September 1943 *Queen Eagle* became *Empress Queen* again and spent the next three years ferrying servicemen between Stranraer and Larne.

Convoys and Submarines

The worst menace faced by the merchant seaman was the submarine. The U-boat most likely to be encountered was the Type VII C, of which 550 or so were built. Carrying a crew of forty-five, it was 67.10m long with a 6.18m beam and was armed with five torpedo tubes and fourteen torpedoes. From 1940 the U-boats could be based in France and Norway, with a shorter passage to the Allied merchant shipping routes.

As in the First World War, the British inaugurated a system of regular convoys (although many vessels continued to voyage independently) with the busiest and most vital convoy routes, those across the North Atlantic, beginning in September 1939 and continuing until May 1945. A convoy was a collection of perhaps twenty to fifty or more merchant ships, of all ages and conditions – many elderly, slow, or with unreliable engines. A Convoy Commander was appointed to try to establish some order, and to keep the vessels together, but final authority lay with the senior officer in the escorting naval vessels. It is worth emphasising the vast quantities of goods carried by these convoys. In February 1943 a convoy of twenty vessels sailed from the eastern United States carrying 5,000 x 2 ½ ton trucks, 2,000 goods trailers, 400 dumper trucks, 4,000 machine guns, 12,000 tons of coal, 16,000 tons of flour, 9,000 tons of sugar, 1,000 tons of soap and eighty aircraft. All arrived safely.

Up to the end of 1943 the German navy's 'B-dienst' service was able to decrypt most of the British signals about convoys and the U-boat controllers were able to direct

63 A wartime convoy, vital to Britain's survival. The first convoy across the North Atlantic was in September 1939 and the last in May 1945.

attacks with some precision. The breakthrough for the Allies came in May 1941 when the British destroyer HMS *Bulldog* sank the German submarine U-110, capturing its code-books and Enigma machine. From then until the end of the war (except for a time in 1942) most German naval signals could be read by the British.

Cardiff Vessels Lost to Enemy Action

Over 100 Cardiff-owned ships were to be destroyed during the war but it is not possible here to name more than a few. Vessels managed by Cardiff firms on behalf of the Ministry of War Transport have not been included.

The first Cardiff loss came five days after war was declared. Tatem's *Winkleigh* (5,055), on an independent voyage from Vancouver to Manchester with a cargo of grain and timber, was torpedoed on 8 September 1939 by the submarine U-48 in the North Atlantic. All thirty-seven men on board were rescued and taken to New York. Ten days later *Vancouver City* (4,739) was torpedoed by U-28 near the end of an independent voyage from Fiji to the United Kingdom with a cargo of sugar. The Reardon Smith vessel went down seventy-five miles west of Milford Haven. Thirty crew members were rescued and landed at Liverpool.

On 22 October *Trevanion* (5,299) – built at Port Glagow and owned by Hain – was intercepted by the battleship *Graf Spee*, which had left Wilhelmshaven two days before

64 The first Cardiff vessel to be sunk in the Second World War was Tatem's *Winkleigh*, lost five days after war was declared. The vessel, on an independent voyage from Vancouver to Manchester carrying gain and timber, was torpedoed in the North Atlantic on 8 September 1939 by the German submarine U-48. All of the crew members were rescued and taken to New York.

war was declared. Before coming across *Trevanion* the *Graf Spee* had accounted for the *Clement* (5,051), *Newton Beach* (4,651), *Ashlea* (4,222), and *Huntsman* (8,196). The *Trevanion* was sunk by explosives. The battleship went on to sink four more merchant ships before the battle of the River Plate in December 1939, after which the *Graf Spee* was scuttled by Captain Hans Langsdorff, who committed suicide.

The *Menin Ridge* (2,470), owned by the Ridge Steamship Co., was built at Burntisland, Fife, in 1924. The ship was sunk on 24 October while carrying 4,200 tons of iron ore in a convoy from Algeria to Port Talbot. Twenty men were lost, and five rescued.

One vessel was lost in November: *Pensilva* (4,258), built in 1929 at Burntisland, and owned by Chellew. Torpedoed and shelled by U-49 on 19 November when in convoy HG 7 (thirty-two ships) completing a passage from Durban to Rouen with 7,000 tons of maize. The crew were rescued by HMS *Echo*. On 7 December *Thomas Walton* (4,460) was sunk. Built in 1917, owned by Frank S. Dawson (Coronation Steamship Company), *Thomas Walton* was torpedoed by U-38 in the North Sea, on an independent voyage – in ballast – from Port Talbot to Narvik. Thirteen crew members died, but twenty-one were rescued and taken to Norway.

During 1940, the first full year of the war, thirty-three Cardiff vessels were sunk, at least one by a disguised surface raider. The German commerce raider *Atlantis* operated under various disguises, posing as an innocent merchant ship but carrying concealed armament of six 5.9-inch guns, four torpedo tubes, nearly 100 mines and a seaplane. *Atlantis* came across Reardon Smith's *King City* on 24 August 1940, in the Indian Ocean to the north of Rodriguez Island. The tramp ship was sunk by gunfire, the crew were taken on board the *Atlantis* and transferred, with 200 other captured seamen, to a captured Yugoslav ship. They were all taken to an Italian prison camp in Somalia.

Two months after this, on 23 October 1940, the German warship *Admiral Scheer,* captained by Theodore Krancke, set off from the Baltic for the North Atlantic. Launched in 1933, *Scheer* could travel 19,000 miles without refuelling, was capable of 26 knots, and carried six 11in and eight 5.9in guns as well as torpedoes and anti-aircraft guns. The Allied convoy HX 84, formed off the coast of Canada, was made up of thirty-eight ships in nine columns which took up ten square miles of the ocean. The only escorting vessel was the *Jervis Bay* (14,164), in peacetime belonging to the Aberdeen and Commonwealth Line, but now conscripted as an Armed Merchant Cruiser. Eighteen years old and with a top speed of 15 knots, the AMC was equipped with seven 5.9in guns. At around 5.00p.m. on 5 November the merchant ships of Convoy HX 84, sighting the *Admiral Scheer*, scattered as fast as they could, but Captain E.S. Fogerty Fegen in *Jervis Bay* made directly for the battleship. It was never going to be any kind of a contest and the converted liner was soon ablaze, unable to steer, with shell holes in the hull, and sinking. Nearly 200 of those on board died, but sixty-five were picked up by a Swedish merchant ship. Captain Fogarty Fegen was awarded a posthumous Victoria Cross 'for valour in challenging hopeless odds and giving his life to save the many ships it was his duty to protect'.

Time had been bought for the cargo ships, but Captain Krancke now hunted them, bombarding and destroying *Beaverford* – seventy-seven men died, *Kenbane Head* – twenty-three died, and *Maidan* – ninety-one died. Two Cardiff ships were sunk by *Admiral Scheer*

65 The German warship *Admiral Scheer*. In November 1940 the *Admiral Scheer* attacked convoy HX 84 in the North Atlantic, sinking the escort vessel – the Armed Merchant Cruiser *Jervis Bay* – and five other ships, including Cardiff's *Fresno City* and *Trewellard*. 400 men died.

on 5 November: *Trewellard* (5,201), built in 1936 at Port Glasgow and owned by Hain, was carrying 7,800 tons of steel and 12 aircraft. Six men died, but there were twenty-five survivors. *Fresno City* (4,955) built in 1929 at Sunderland, and owned by Reardon Smith, was carrying 8,000 tons of maize. Found by *Scheer* at about 9.00p.m, *Fresno City* was sunk by seven shells fired at close range. The crew took to the two undamaged lifeboats and were later picked up, the master's boat having sailed 200 miles before being sighted by a Greek vessel. *Admiral Scheer* went on to sink another nine Allied merchant ships, before being finished off by bombs at Kiel in 1944.

Other Cardiff ships lost in November 1940 were:

11 November *Trebartha* (4,597). Built in 1920 at South Shields, owned by Hain. The vessel was bombed four miles south-east of Aberdeen, and set on fire. After being beached, she broke in two, and was abandoned.

21 November *Daydawn* (4,769). Owned by Claymore, the vessel was being built at Sunderland when the war began. Sunk with a cargo of nearly 7,000 tons of coal while with convoy OB 244 (forty-six ships) which left Liverpool on 17 November. The convoy was forced to disperse on 22 November, when three ships were sunk. *Daydawn* was torpedoed by U-103. Thirty-eight men died and four survived.

22 November *Justitia* (4,562). Built in 1935 at Burntisland, owned by Chellew, and with a cargo of 5,200 tons of timber and 2,300 tons of steel. In convoy SC 11 which had left Sydney, Cape Breton, on 9 November. Of the thirty-four merchant vessels, seven were sunk by U-100, including *Justitia,* from which thirteen men died and twenty-six survived.

22 November *Bradfyne* (4,740). Built at Burntisland in 1935, owned by Reardon Smith. Like *Justitia* part of convoy SC 11, *Bradfyne* was carrying a cargo of 8,000 tons of grain when torpedoed by U-100 south-east of Rockall. Thirty-nine died but four men were rescued by a Norwegian ship and taken to Belfast.

24 November *Behar* (6,100). Built in 1928 at Greenock and owned by Hain, the ship hit a mine, and was deliberately run on to the rocks at Great Castle Head, near the entrance to Milford Haven. All the crew survived.

28 November *St Elwyn* (4,940). Built at Sunderland in 1938, owned by B&S Shipping. Carrying coal from Hull to Santos in convoy OB 249 (fifty-four ships). Torpedoed by U-103, 500 miles east of the Bishop Rock. Twenty-four died but sixteen were rescued by *Leeds City* and landed at Gourock.

In the next year of the war, 1941, thirty-one Cardiff vessels were sunk, eight of them in June: *Prince Rupert City* (4,745) – most of the crew were rescued, but four died; *Trecarrel* (5,271) – four of the crew were lost; *Sacramento Valley* (4,573) – three men died; *Tregarthen* (5,201) – of the crew of forty-five, there were no survivors; *Trevarrack* (5,270) – all the forty-four crew members died; *Tresillian* (4,573) – all the crew were saved; *St Lindsay* (5,370) – all forty-three members of the crew died; *Trelissick* (5,265) – two of the crew were lost.

On 7 December 1941 the Japanese, with no declaration of war, bombed US warships at Pearl Harbor. Four days later Germany declared war on the United States.

Twenty-four Cardiff ships were destroyed in 1942, including *Llandilo* (4,966) on 2 November. Built at Sunderland in 1928, owned by Evan Thomas Radcliffe,

66 British merchant seamen rescued by a US coastguard vessel.

torpedoed by U-172 while voyaging alone New York to Trinidad to Durban to Bombay with 9,000 tons of US military stores. The vessel went down in the South Atlantic, south-east of St Helena. Twenty-four men died; twenty were rescued by a Norwegian ship and taken to Port of Spain.

Eight days later (10 November) came the sinking of *Garlinge* (2,012). Built in 1918 at Chepstow, and now owned by Constants, the elderly vessel was carrying 2,700 tons of coal in a small convoy of four ships supporting 'Operation Torch', the Allied landings in North Africa. The convoy left Gibraltar on 7 November, with an escort of five armed trawlers. The *Garlinge* was equipped with a 12 pounder gun, four 20mm Oerlikon guns and two machine guns. Straggling behind the rest, the Cardiff vessel was torpedoed just after midnight by U-81, twenty miles off the Algerian coast. Twenty-five men died, but fifteen survivors were picked up, after some hours on life rafts, by one of the escort vessels.

Fifteen vessels were lost in 1943, among them:

Clarissa Radcliffe (5,754). Launched at Stockton-on-Tees in 1915 as the *Windsor*, and now owned by Evan Thomas Radcliffe. Part of convoy SC 122 (fifty-one ships), the vessel was carrying iron ore. The convoy, deploying into thirteen parallel columns, left New York on 5 March 1943, with an ocean escort of two destroyers, a frigate, five Flower class corvettes and an American Armed Trawler. Three days out of New York the vessels were dispersed by a gale and the *Clarissa Radcliffe* was not seen again. Probably sunk by submarine U-633, all fifty-five men on board died. The convoy lost eight merchant ships and the Armed Trawler.

Nailsea Court (4,946). Built at Sunderland in 1936, owned by Evans and Reid. The vessel had travelled from Beira to New York, and was now part of convoy SC 121 (fifty-seven ships) which had left New York on 5 March. *Nailsea Court* was torpedoed south of Reykjavik by U-229. Forty-three men died. One survivor was picked up by the convoy rescue ship *Melrose Abbey* and put ashore at Gourock on 13 March. The other three survivors were rescued by Royal Canadian Navy corvette *Dauphin* (925) and taken to Northern Ireland.

Hadleigh (5,222). Built in 1930 on the Tees, owned by W.J. Tatem. On the way, in ballast, from Algiers to Gibraltar as part of convoy ET 114 (thirty ships). Torpedoed by U-77 on 16 March *Hadleigh* was damaged and the crew abandoned ship, but they went back on board and their vessel was taken in tow by the tug *Restive*. Beached at Mers el Kebir, *Hadleigh* was declared a total loss. Two crew members died and fifty were taken on board the destroyer HMS *Tynedale*.

'Victory in Europe Day' (VE Day) was celebrated on 8 May 1945, and 'Victory over Japan' (VJ Day) was declared to be 15 August 1945. Before hostilities ended seven more Cardiff vessels had been lost and one, the twenty-year-old *Vera Radcliffe*, was sold to the government and sunk to make part of a harbour built on the Normandy coast.

During the war about 60 per cent of Cardiff's pre-war fleet had been destroyed. The German attempts to cut the British lifelines cost them 720 U-boats and the lives of 30,000 men. Britain lost 1,600 merchant ships and over 30,000 merchant seamen.

11

THE YEARS OF DECLINE

In 1948 the Bute Docks were taken into public ownership, to be controlled by the Docks and Inland Waterways Executive of the British Transport Commission. The Chief Docks Manager for south Wales, to be based at Cardiff, was made responsible for the management of the docks at Barry, Cardiff and Penarth, Newport, Port Talbot and Swansea.

At Cardiff the two original Bute docks – West and East – were by now used only by smaller vessels. Neale and West's trawlers were still operating from the West Dock. A unit of the Royal Naval Reserve was based at the East Dock with, from the early 1950s, their

67 An aerial view of Cardiff Docks in 1948.

River class frigate HMS *Derg*, later to be renamed HMS *Cambria*. (*Derg* was one of the ships assembled at Tokyo Bay for the surrender of the Japanese armed forces in 1945. The vessel was broken up in 1960.) The south side of the Queen Alexandra Dock was used for loading coal, while the north side was designated for general cargoes.

Roath Dock, in addition to handling coal, was still the dock for Spillers, whose cargoes could be discharged straight into a large grain silo and then transferred into the flour mill. The Dowlais Works (by now Guest Keen and Baldwin's) was next door to the wharf where iron ore was discharged and the works' products loaded.

Overall, the Bute Docks' facilities were still considerable, with twenty-two hoists and two conveyor belts for loading coal, nearly a hundred cranes, including a floating crane which could lift 100 tons, a large cold store and twenty-three transit sheds. And, of course, miles of railway lines.

68
Discharging
iron ore at
Roath Dock.

Ship-repairing could be done in the three Mount Stuart dry docks. C.H. Bailey's owned three dry docks and, in addition, there was the Bute West Graving Dock, and the two dry docks and a pontoon belonging to the Channel Dry Dock Co. The dock authorities operated a dry dock and gridiron at Roath Basin.

But traffic through the docks had diminished: in the last full year before the Second World War, 4,241 vessels (with a total net registered tonnage of 2,623,442) entered Cardiff Docks. In 1947, the last full year before nationalisation, there were 2,370 vessels (net registered tonnage 1,383,883). There had been a disastrous fall in Cardiff's exports: in 1938 exports of coal, coke and patent fuel amounted to 5,229,095 tons. In 1947 only 736,174 tons were exported.

Penarth Dock was closed again at the end of the war, except for ship-repairs and for laying up, and in 1949 two four-masted steel barques could be seen taking advantage of this facility. The *Passat* (3,091) had left South Australia with a cargo of grain, and took 110 days to make her way to Queenstown, before going on to Barry and Penarth. Built in 1911 by Blöhm and Voss of Hamburg, the vessel had been built for the nitrate trade. After her sojourn at Penarth, *Passat* became a sail-training and merchant ship, and is now preserved at Trävemunde in north Germany. *Pamir* (3,020) was built by Blöhm and Voss in 1905, also for the nitrate trade. From 1931 the vessel was in Finnish ownership, engaged in carrying grain from Australia until seized in New Zealand during the Second

69 Penarth Dock, 1948.

World War. With Finnish owners again from 1948, her last voyage before arriving at Penarth was, like *Pamir*'s, from South Australia. Sold for breaking up, *Passat* escaped that fate and became instead a sail-training ship. On 10 August 1956 the vessel sailed from Buenos Aires for Hamburg with 3,800 tons of barley, and a crew of eighty-six. On 21 September *Passat* sank in a storm, 600 miles from the Azores. There were only six survivors.

The 1950s

The aircraft carrier *Campania* visited Cardiff from 31 July to 11 August 1951, as part of the 'Festival of Britain,' which was intended as a celebration of British achievements. The vessel had been built (converted from the partly completed hull of a refrigerated merchant ship) by Harland and Wolff in Belfast. Launched on 17 June 1943, it was 164.5m long, with a 21.3m beam and a draught of 7m. HMS *Campania* had been laid up in the Gareloch for four years before being lent to the Festival of Britain as an 'exhibition ship'.

Over 8 million people visited the South Bank Exhibition in London, and across Britain there were government-sponsored exhibitions and arts festivals, with 2,000 cities, towns and villages organising local activities. In Cardiff the main events were a 'Pageant of Wales,' the St Fagans Folk Festival and the arrival of the *Campania*, which was visiting ten ports in five months. The aim of this 'Sea Travelling Exhibition' (and its counterpart the Land Travelling Exhibition) was to transport a version of the South Bank Exhibition, with its themes of 'The Land of Britain', 'Discovery' and 'The People at Home'. Of interest to south Walians was the section about minerals: 'Coal – the prize gem: and steel, the development of which is, of course, a British achievement'. *Campania* was visited by 104,391 people during the twelve days at Queen Alexandra Dock.

Many of those visitors to the Festival Ship may have been conscious that the Bute Docks were not what they were, but none of them would have been able to predict the extent of the changes which lay ahead. New methods of cargo handling began to be introduced in the 1950s, with the development of 'palletization' – stacking and moving goods on wooden pallets – making for easier storage, loading and unloading. At sea, there was increasing use of the bulk carrier, which had engines aft and was able to carry considerably more cargo than its traditional counterpart. The total traffic (measured in tons) being moved through Cardiff Docks had decreased by 50 per cent compared with two decades earlier, and now many famous Cardiff shipping companies began to go under:

The Claymore Shipping Co. had no vessels at the end of the war, but began acquiring ships from 1947 – first a Liberty ship which was renamed *Daybeam* (7,233), then the former *Empire Nerissa* which became *Daydawn* (7,036) and, finally, the *Dayrose* (7,036). All Claymore's vessels had been sold by 1956.

In 1947 Chellew bought the four-year-old *Pentire*, formerly the Liberty ship *Samnebra*, built by Bethlehem-Fairfield at Baltimore, Maryland. The company ceased to exist in 1954. By the following year the *Pentire* had been renamed the *Cuaco* and was sailing under the flag of Panama.

Care left the scene in 1955 – they had been running the Care Lines *Porthrepta* (643) and the R.P. Care *Carbis Bay* (752).

At the end of the war Neale & West's surviving vessels were *Akita*, *Hatsuse*, *Muroto*, *Nodzu*, *Oku*, *Sasebo*, *Sata* and *Yashima*. The *Aby* was acquired in 1945 and the *St Botolph* in 1946 – built by Cook, Wellington and Gemmel of Beverley. The rest of the fleet was made up of second-hand vessels: *Braemar* (built in 1927), *Fort Dee* (built in 1929) and *Warlord* (built in 1914). But costs were rising, fish were scarcer, and the trawlers had to make much longer voyages to their fishing grounds. The end of Cardiff as a fishing port came in 1956, when all the vessels were sold.

Morel Ltd lost four vessels in the Second World War: *Allende* (3,177), *Beignon* (3,004), *Jersey* (3,032) and *Pontypridd* (2,736). Their fleet by 1948 consisted of *Nolisement* (3,174) – built in 1928, *Catrine* (3,004) – built in 1940, and *Jersey May* (4,421) – built at Baltimore in 1944 as the *Samluzon*. *Nolisement* and *Jersey May* were sold in 1950 and three new vessels were bought in 1953/54: *Jersey Spray* (3,015), *Jersey Dawn* (2,879), and *Jersey Mist* (3,003). The whole fleet of four vessels was sold in 1956.

Lovering & Sons, ship-owners since 1936, traded on the shorter routes – around the British Isles and to European ports. After the war they bought, in 1947, the five-year-old Lowestoft-built *Empire Punch*, followed in 1948 by *Fennel*, in 1949 by *Staniel* and in 1951 by *Petertown*. There were no survivors when the *Teasel* was lost in the Irish Sea in January 1948. All vessels had been sold by the end of the 1950s, with the *Staniel*, after being damaged by fire off Lowestoft, sent for scrap.

The 1960s

The Ely River coal tips closed in 1962 and Penarth Dock in 1963, the same year in which the British Transport Docks Board was set up. The Bute West Dock was closed down in January 1964, after 125 years. The British Transport Docks Board decided that south Wales coal would in future be exported through Barry and Swansea, and on 25 August 1964 the coaster *Farringay* left Queen Alexandra Dock with what was regarded as the final cargo of coal to leave Cardiff (although very small quantities have continued to be imported and exported). The railway tracks, sidings and coal tips became redundant, there was no traffic on the Rhymney Railway lines into the docks and in 1968 the Taff Vale Railway's line to the Roath Dock was shut.

The beginning of containerisation in the mid-1960s had enormous implications for the future of ports, methods of cargo-handling and storage, and the design and size of ships. Cargoes came to be transported in standardised steel containers instead of in thousands of boxes, crates or sacks. Loading and unloading became much quicker, more easily mechanised, employed fewer dock workers, and there was less chance of damage. Fewer warehouses were needed, because containers could be stacked in the open air. Ships grew ever larger, many docks were now too small, and the first British ports designed to handle containers opened in 1968 at Felixtowe and Tilbury.

More Cardiff shipping companies ceased trading. Frederick Jones's *Tintern Abbey* voyaged to the Mediterranean, usually going out in ballast, and bringing back iron ore,

70 Penarth Dock, with vessels laid up. Most of the coal tips have gone and there is little sign of any activity.

phosphate and esparto grass. With the end of the Korean war freight rates plummeted, and *Tintern Abbey* was idle in Barry Docks for three years, until being sold in 1960. Frederick Jones died on the December 1961, at the age of ninety-three.

W.H. Seager & Sons had started in 1904 with the *Tempus* (2,981). After the Second World War they operated two ships: *Beatus* (7,128), bought in 1947, had been built as *Fort Tremblant* at Victoria, British Columbia. The vessel was sold in 1955. The steamer *Amicus* (7,125) was acquired in 1946 – it was formerly the *Empire Noble*, built at Barrow in 1944. Although often laid up at Cardiff, *Amicus* spent some time in 1962 working between China and Cuba, before being sold in 1963.

At the end of the war B&S Shipping owned, in the South American Saint Line: *St Clears* (4,312), *St Merriel* (5,348), and *St Rosario* (4,312) and in the Shakespear Shipping Co., *St Elwyn* (5,199). By 1948 the fleet had expanded to ten, including two Liberty ships named *St Arvans* and *St Helena* and the *St Margaret* (7,015) which, as the *Empire Cameron*, the company had managed for the Ministry of War Transport. Two newly built vessels arrived in 1948, the *St Essylt* (6,855) and *St Thomas* (6,355). For some years the company's ships were employed on a liner service from south Wales ports to the River Plate, with calls at Antwerp, Bremen and Hamburg. The firm closed its Cardiff office in 1961, and the last vessel was sold in 1965.

John Cory & Sons lost the three ships with which they started the war and one bought as a replacement – *Start Point* – had been sunk on her second trip. After the war they chartered the steamship *Fort Mattagami* (7,150) for two years and then, in 1948, bought the *Ramillies* (7,174) followed in 1954 by the nine-year-old *Ravenshoe* (7,295) The company, which had been in business since the 1870s, ceased ship-owning in 1966.

The 1970s

The Bute East Dock closed in January 1970, the railway sidings and tips were removed, and by September 1970 the West Dock – opened 131 years earlier – had been filled in.

W.J. Tatem had been killed in 1942 during an air raid on Weston-super-Mare. His firm had acquired since the end of the war: 1946 – *Chulmleigh* (5,349), launched as *Empire Northfleet* for the Ministry of War Transport; 1947 *Lord Glanely* (5,640); 1957 *Filleigh* (5,668); 1960 *Glanely* (8,261). All had been sold by the end of the 1960s. *Landwade* (7,856) was bought in 1961 and *Exning* (7,465) – the firm's last – in 1965; by 1973 both had gone.

Constants was a London-based firm which had set up Constants (South Wales) Ltd in 1929. After forty years at Cardiff, by the end of the 1960s they were trading with *Beltinge, Garlinge, Lotlinge, Lyminge* and *Susan Constant*, which had all had been disposed of by 1976.

The East Moors (Dowlais) Steelworks, which had opened on 4 February 1891, closed down on 28 April 1978, with consequent loss of trade through the docks, although a new rod mill was to be opened at a later date.

The 1980s

Three more famous companies ceased to own ships in the 1980s – P&A Campbell, Evan Thomas Radcliffe and Reardon Smith.

71 P&A Campbell tried out a Hovercraft service between Penarth and Weston-super-Mare in July and August 1963.

During the 1950s, vessels of P&A Campbell were sold off one by one, and from 23 July to 30 August 1963 Campbells experimented with a 27 ton SRN2 Hovercraft to provide a passenger service between Penarth and Weston-super-Mare. The *Cardiff Queen* was offered for sale in 1966 and the *Bristol Queen* was taken out of service a year later. Two motor vessels, *Westward Ho* and *Balmoral*, continued until 1980.

In the post-war period, until 1970, Evan Thomas Radcliffe owned a fleet of five, including *Llanishen* (20,976), a tanker built on the Tyne – 193m long x 19.5m beam; *Llantrisant* (6,171) – built by Bartram & Sons at Sunderland; *Hamilton* (13,186), a Belgian-built tanker; *Llangorse* (21,840), a tanker built on the Tees by the Furness Shipbuilding Co. and *Llanwern* (9,229), built by Bartram. By 1983, when the company closed down, there were only two small vessels, the *Radcliffe Trader* (622), twenty-seven years old, and the *Radcliffe Venturer* (504), seventeen years old.

In the years after the war the Reardon Smith Line owned seventeen vessels, but by 1965 there were eleven, including their first two bulk carriers, which had been built on the Clyde by Fairfields and named *Australian City* (18,461) and *Eastern City* (18,461). During the early 1970s Reardon Smith's began to diversify, taking an interest in oil exploration, but also acquiring three more bulk carriers: *Eastern City* (35,677) from a Danish yard and two built at Sunderland – *Orient City* (39,200) and *Welsh City* (39,200). From around the mid-1970s vessels were sold, and the firm went into voluntary liquidation in May 1985.

'Associated British Ports' was established in 1981 to take over the facilities previously run by the British Transport Docks Board. At Cardiff the new body acquired docks whose chief exports were grain, wire and steel products, and scrap metal. Imports included timber from Scandinavia, Russia and North America, fruit from Israel and South Africa, and dairy products from New Zealand.

72 Reardon Smith's *Leeds City*, built in 1955 by William Doxford & Sons, Sunderland. In 1967 it was sold to Greek owners and operated under several names until laid up in 1982.

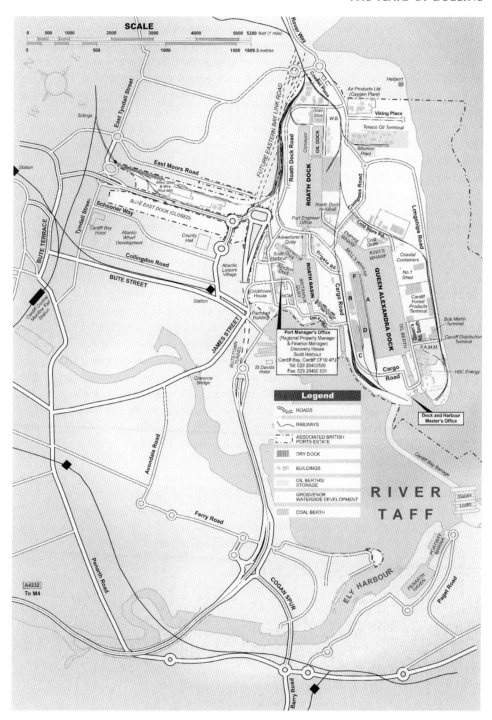

73 The port of Cardiff, under the management of Associated British Ports.

Six years later, on 3 April 1987, Cardiff Bay Development Corporation came into being, having been set up by the government as part of an initiative to bring life back to run-down areas of cities. The Development Corporation was charged with improving the Cardiff dockland – an area of 1,100 hectares – and providing 30,000 jobs, 6,000 dwellings, and attracting 2 million visitors a year by the millennium.

At the Millennium

Construction of a barrage began on 25 May 1994, and was completed on 4 November 1999. The Cardiff Bay Development Corporation was wound up on 31 March 2000 and next day the Cardiff Harbour Authority came into being, assuming responsibility for the new Cardiff Bay lake and barrage, the graving docks and the Oval Basin. At Penarth, most of the dock had been filled in, and the rest of it turned into a marina. The coal-tips and other dockside facilities were replaced by houses. Two preserved vessels – the motor vessel *Balmoral* and the paddle steamer *Waverley* – made seasonal excursions from Penarth pier.

At the millennium, shipping management companies had not entirely disappeared from Cardiff, and the city was the headquarters of Graig Shipping, started in October 1919 by Idwal Williams, and Charles M. Willie Shipping, whose first vessel was bought in 1929. The Docks themselves, and twenty other ports throughout Britain, were managed by Associated British Ports. The Bute Docks remaining in use in the year 2000 were the Queen Alexandra and Roath Docks and the Roath Basin, which were visited by an average of about ten vessels a week. The port was the base for the Royal Mail Ship *St Helena* (6,767), which carried passengers and cargo to the British Overseas Territory of St Helena in the South Atlantic, as well as to Ascension Island, Cape Town and – once a year – to Tristan da Cunha.

80 per cent of the cargo handled by the port was inbound (a complete reversal of the situation in the docks' heyday) and included oil products, containers, iron and steel, and dry bulks. Outward-bound cargoes included steel (wire rod, reinforcing bar and merchant bar) and coal – reminders of past times when Cardiff flourished as the port for the upland ironworks and the coal-mining valleys.

74 Handling a cargo of steel.

75 Timber being discharged at the Queen Alexandra Dock.

BIBLIOGRAPHY

Appleyard, H.S. and Heaton, P.M. (1981) *The Baron Glanely of St Fagans and W.J. Tatem Ltd* (World Ship Society).

Asteris, Michael (1986) 'The rise and decline of south Wales coal exports 1870–1930' *Welsh Historical Review* 13, 24–43.

Baber, C. and Williams L.J. (Eds) (1986) *Modern South Wales: Essays in Economic History* (Cardiff University).

Balfour, Campbell (1970) 'Captain Tupper and the 1911 seamen's strike in Cardiff' *Morgannwg* XIV, 62–80.

Ballinger, John (Ed.) (1896) *Cardiff: An Illustrated Handbook* (Cardiff: Western Mail).

Ballinger, John (1908) *Guide to Cardiff: City and Port* (Cardiff: Rees Electric Printing Works).

Batchelor, K.B. (1975) *John Batchelor: The Friend of Freedom* (Holt Magazine).

Beche, H. de la and Playfair, L. (1851) *Third Report on the coals suited to the steam navy* (HMSO).

Bennett, Peter and Jenkins, David (1994) *Welsh Ports of the Great Western Railway* (National Museum of Wales).

Bestic, A.A. (1957) *Kicking Canvas* (Evans Bros).

Bird, John (1987) *The Diaries of John Bird of Cardiff* (Edited by Hilary M. Thomas for the South Wales Record Society).

Boughey, Joseph (Ed.) (1998) *Hadfield's British Canals* (8th Ed.) (Sutton).

Boyns, T., Thomas D. and Baber C. (1980) 'The iron, steel and tinplate industries, 1750–1914' in John A.H. and Williams G. (Eds) *Glamorgan County History* Vol. V, 97–154. (Glamorgan County History Trust).

British Transport Commission (1948) *South Wales Ports* (Cardiff: Office of the Chief Docks Manager).

British vessels lost at sea 1914-1918 (Patrick Stephens 1988. Facsimile of the official publication of 1919).

British vessels lost at sea 1939-45 (Patrick Stephens 1976. Facsimile of the official publication of 1947).

Burge, Alan (1992) 'The 1926 General Strike in Cardiff' *Llafur* 6, No.1, 42–61.

Burwash, Dorothy (1947) *English Merchant Shipping 1460–1540* (David and Charles).

Buxton I. L. (1993) 'The development of the merchant ship 1880–1990' *The Mariner's Mirror* 79 (1) 71–82.

Campbell, P&A, (1923) *Bristol Channel District Guide* (41st edition) (c.1923).

Cardiff City Council (1935) *The City, Port and District of Cardiff* (Cardiff: Western Mail).

Chapman, W.G. (1927) *Twixt rail and sea. A book of docks seaports and shipping for boys of all ages* (H.N. Appleby and Great Western Railway).

Chappell, Edgar L. (1939) *History of the Port of Cardiff* (Cardiff: Priory Press).

Clark, G.T. (1883) *Some account of Sir Robert Mansel and Admiral Sir Thomas Button* (Dowlais).

Clayton, H.W. (1865) *Clayton's Annual Register of Shipping* (reproduced by Merseyside Maritime Museum 2002).

Collard, Chris (1999) *A Dangerous Occupation. White Funnels – Volume 3. A Story of Paddle Steamers in the First World War* (Cardiff: Wheelhouse Books).

Collard, Chris (2003) *On Admiralty Service: P&A Campbell in the Second World War* (Tempus).

Coombes, Nigel (1990) *Passenger Steamers of the Bristol Channel: A Pictorial Record* (Truro: Twelveheads Press).

— (1995) *White Funnel Magic* (Truro: Twelveheads Press).

Craig, R.S. (1980) 'The ports and shipping 1750–1914' in John, A.H. and Williams, G. (Eds) *Glamorgan County History* Volume V, 465–518 (Glamorgan County History Trust).

— (1986) *Trade and shipping in south Wales – the Radcliffe Company, 1882–1921* in Baber, C. and Williams, L.J. (1986).

Crawshay, Richard *The Letterbook of Richard Crawshay 1788–1797.* Calendered by Chris Evans (Cardiff: South Wales Record Society 1990).

Daunton, M.J. (1977) *Coal Metropolis, Cardiff 1870–1914* (Leicester University Press).

— (1978) 'The Coal Trimmers Union, 1888–1914' *Llafur* 2 (3), 10–23.

— (1978) 'Jack Ashore: Seamen in Cardiff before 1914' *Welsh Historical Review* 9, 176–203.

— (1988) 'Coal to Capital: Cardiff since 1839' in Morgan, Prys (Ed.) *Glamorgan County History* Vol. VI (Glamorgan History Trust).

Davies, John (1981) *Cardiff and the Marquesses of Bute* (University of Wales Press).

Denning, R.T.W. (1995) *The Diary of William Thomas of Michaelston-super-Ely, 1762–1795* (South Wales Record Society).

De Salis, H.R. (1904) *Bradshaw's Canals and Navigable Rivers of England and Wales* (Henry Blacklock & Co.).

Edwards, Bernard (1987) *They sank the Red Dragon* (Cardiff: GPC Books).

Elphick, Peter (1999) *Life Line: The Merchant Navy at War 1939–1945* (Chatham).

Elsas, Madelaine (Ed.) (1960) *Iron in the Making: Dowlais Iron Company Letters 1782–1860* (Glamorgan County Council and Guest Keen Iron and Steel Company).

Evans, Catherine; Dodsworth, Steve; Barnett, Julie (1984) *Below the Bridge: a photo – historical survey of Cardiff's docklands to 1983* (National Museum of Wales).

Evans, Neil (1980) 'The south Wales race riots of 1919' *Llafur* 3 (No. 1), 5–29.

Evans, Neil (1983) 'The south Wales race riots of 1919: a documentary postscript' *Llafur* 3 (No. 4), 76–87.

Evans, Neil (1985) 'The Welsh Victorian city: the middle class and civic and national consciousness in Cardiff 1850 -1914' *Welsh Historical Review* 12, 350 – 387.

Evans, Neil (1988) 'A tidal wave of impatience: the Cardiff General Strike of 1911' in Jenkins, G.H. and Smith J.B. *Politics and Society in Wales* (University of Wales Press).

Farr, Grahame E. (1956) *West Country Passenger Steamers* (Richard Tilling).

Farr, Grahame E. (1967) *Wreck and Rescue in the Bristol Channel* (Truro: Bradford Barton).

Foster, Cecil (1924) *1700 Miles in Open Boats* (Martin Hopkinson & Company).

Gibbs, J.M. (1982) *Morels of Cardiff: the history of a family shipping firm* (National Museum of Wales).

Gray, Leonard and Lingwood, John (1975) *The Doxford Turret Ships* (Kendal: World Ship Society).

Green, Colin (1999) *Severn Traders: The West Country Trows and Trowmen* (Lydney: Black Dwarf).

Greenhill, Basil (1988) *The Merchant Schooners* (Conway).

Griffiths, R.A. (1984) 'Medieval Severnside: the Welsh connection' in Davies R.R. *et al.* (Eds) *Welsh Society and Nationhood: Historical Essays Presented to Glanmor Williams* (University of Wales Press).

Gross, Joseph (Ed.) (2001) *The Diary of Charles Wood of Cyfarthfa Ironworks, Merthyr Tydfil 1766–1767* (Merton Priory Press).

Gruffydd, K. Lloyd (2003) 'Piracy, privateering and maritime Wales during the later Middle Ages' (part 1) *Maritime Wales* 24, 24–40.

Gruffydd, K. Lloyd (2004) 'Piracy, privateering and maritime Wales during the later Middle Ages' (part 2) *Maritime Wales* 25, 10–20.

Hadfield, Charles (1967) *The Canals of South Wales and the Border* (David and Charles).

Handley, Chris (2001) *Maritime Activities of the Somerset and Dorset Railway* (Bath: Millstream Books).

Heaton, P.M. (1983) *The Abbey Line: History of a Cardiff Shipping Venture* (Risca: Starling Press).

— (1984) *Reardon Smith Line: the history of a south Wales shipping venture* (Risca: Starling Press).

— (1985) *The South American Saint Line* (Risca: Starling Press).

— (1985) *Welsh Blockade Runners of the Spanish Civil War* (Risca: Starling Press).

— (1987) *Tatems of Cardiff* (Risca: Starling Press).

— (1989) *Welsh Shipping: Forgotten Fleets* (Risca: Starling Press).

Hill, John C.G. *Shipshape and Bristol Fashion* (Liverpool: The Journal of Commerce and Shipping Telegraph).

Hobbs, J.S. (Ed.) (1859) *The Bristol Channel Pilot* (Charles Wilson).

Hurd, Archibald (1922) *The Triumph of the Tramp Ship* (Cassell).

Hussey, David (2000) *Coastal and River Trade in Pre-industrial England: Bristol and its region 1680–1730* (University of Exeter Press).

Ince, Laurence (2001) *Neath Abbey and the Industrial Revolution* (Tempus).

James, Brian Ll. (Ed.) (1983) *Morganiae Archaiographia: A Book of the Antiquities of Glamorganshire*, by Rice Merrick (South Wales Record Society).

Jeffries, David Emrys (1978) *Maritime Memories of Cardiff* (Risca: Starling Press).

Jenkins, David (1984–7) 'Cardiff Tramps, Cardi Crews: Cardiganshire shipowners and seamen in Cardiff *c.*1870–1950' *Ceredigion* X, 405–430.

— (1986) 'Sir William Reardon Smith and the St Just Steamship Co. Ltd (1912–22)' *Maritime Wales* 10, 45–62.

— (1991) *Owen and Watkin Williams of Cardiff. The Golden Cross Line.* (Kendal: World Ship Society).

— (1992) 'The Chellew Steam Navigation Company Limited: A note on some Welsh connections' *Maritime Wales* 15, 82–84.

— (1997) *Shipowners of Cardiff: a class by themselves* (University of Wales Press/National Museums and Galleries of Wales).

Jenkins, J. Geraint (1980) 'Cardiff shipowners' *Maritime Wales* 5, 115–131.

— (1982) *Evan Thomas Radcliffe: a Cardiff shipowning company* (National Museum of Wales).

Jenkins, J. Geraint. and Jenkins, D. (1986) *Cardiff Shipowners* (National Museum of Wales).

Jenkins, J. Geraint (1987) 'The fishing ports of Wales' *Maritime Wales* 11, 74–96.

Jenkins, J. Geraint (1991) *The Inshore Fishermen of Wales* (University of Wales Press).

Johnson, A.M. (1995) *Scott of the Antarctic and Cardiff* (The Captain Scott Society).

Jones, Stephen (1972) 'Blood red roses: the supply of merchant seamen in the nineteenth century' *The Mariner's Mirror* 58 (4), 429–442.

Jordan, Roger (1999) *The World's Merchant Fleets 1939* (Chatham).

Kirkaldy, Adam W., (1914) *British Shipping: Its history, organisation and importance* (Kegan Paul).

Kverndal, Ronald (1986) *Seamen's Missions: Their origin and early growth* (Pasadena: William Carey Library).

Lewis, E.A. (1927) *The Welsh Port Books 1550–1603* (Cymmrodorion Record Series No. XII) (Honourable Society of Cymmrodorion).

Lewis, E.D. (1959) *The Rhondda Valleys: A Study in industrial development 1800 to the present – day* (Phoenix House).

Lloyd's List & Shipping Gazette (27 and 28 August and 5 September 1923) 'The story of the *Trevessa's* boats. Logs of the Master and Chief Officer'.

Lund, Alfred (1989) *The Red Duster: An account of the living and working conditions in the Merchant Navy in peacetime and in war* (Whitby Press).

MacGregor, David R. (1984) *Merchant Sailing Ships 1815–1850* (Conway).

MacRae, J.A. and Waine C.V. (1990) *The Steam Collier Fleets* (Waine Research Publications).

McGrail, Sean and Roberts, Owain (1999) 'A Romano-British boat from the shores of the Severn estuary' *The Mariner's Mirror* 85 (2) 133–146.

McConnochie, John (1876) 'The Bute Docks, Cardiff and the mechanical appliances for shipping coal' *Proceedings of the Institution of Mechanical Engineers at Cardiff 1874* (Cardiff: William Lewis, Steam Printer, Duke Street).

Mathew, David (1924) 'The Cornish and Welsh pirates in the reign of Elizabeth' *English Historical Review* XXXIX, 337–348.

Matthews, J.H. (1898–1911) *Cardiff Records* (six volumes).

Mitchell, B.R. (1971) *Abstract of British Historical Statistics* (Cambridge University Press).

Morgan, D.J. (1986) 'Disaster in the Bristol Channel: the great gale of 1908' *Maritime Wales* 10, 63–68.

Morgan, David Jeffrey (1989) 'Boom and slump – shipowning at Cardiff 1919–21' *Maritime Wales* 12, 126–151.

Morgan, Dennis (1991) *The Cardiff Story* (Cowbridge: D. Brown & Sons).

— (1998) *Cardiff: a city at war* (Published by the author).

Morris, M.G.R. (Ed.) (1998) *Romilly's Visits to Wales 1827–1854* (Gomer Press).

Morris, J.H. and Williams, L.J. (1958) *The South Wales Coal Industry 1841–1875* (University of Wales Press).

Mote, Gordon (1986) *The Westcountrymen: a register and record of the Westcountry trading ketches and Severn trows 1780–1986* (Bideford: Badger Books).

Mountford, Eric (1987) *The Cardiff Railway* (Oxford: Oakwood Press).

O'Donoghue, K.J. and Appleyard, H.S. (1986) *Hain of St Ives* (World Ship Society).

O'Neill, Dan (2001) *Tiger Bay and the Docks* (Derby: Breedon Books).

Perkins, John W. (1984) *The Building Stones of Cardiff* (University College Cardiff).

Pierce, Gwynnedd O. (2002) *Place Names in Glamorgan* (Merton Priory Press).

Pollins, Harold (1980) 'The development of transport 1750–1914' in John, A.H. and Williams, G. (Eds) *Glamorgan County History* Volume V, 421–464. (Glamorgan County History Trust).

Pope, Dudley (1977) *Harry Morgan's Way: The biography of Sir Henry Morgan 1635–1684* (Secker and Warburg).

Potts, C.R. (1996) *The GWR and the General Strike* (Oakwood Press).

Powell, Terry (2000) *Staith to Conveyor: An illustrated history of coal shipping machinery* (Chilton Ironworks).

Redknap, Mark (1997–8) 'An archaeological and historical context for the medieval Magor Pill boat' *Maritime Wales* 19, 9–29.

Redknap, Mark (2000) *Vikings in Wales: An Archaeological Quest* (National Museums and Galleries of Wales).

Rees, William (1969) *Cardiff: A History of the City* (Cardiff Corporation).

Riches, T.H. and Heywood, T.E. (1906) 'Mechanical appliances used in the shipping of coal at Penarth Dock' *Proceedings of the Institution of Mechanical Engineers* July 1906, 423–433.

Roberts, Owain and McGrail, Sean (2002) 'A Romano – British boat recovered from a site in Gwent' *Maritime Wales* 23, 32–36.

Roberts, Stephen K. (Ed.) (1999) *The Letter-Book of John Byrd: Customs Collector in South-East Wales 1648–80* (South Wales Record Society).

Robinson, W.R.B. (1970) 'The establishment of the royal customs in Glamorganshire and Monmouthshire under Elizabeth I' *Bulletin of the Board of Celtic Studies* 23 (4).

— (1972) 'Dr. Phaer's report on the harbours and customs administration of Wales' *Bulletin of the Board of Celtic Studies* XXIV, 493 ff.

Rodger N.A.M. (1997) *The Safeguard of the Sea: a Naval History of Great Britain. Volume I* (HarperCollins).

Roese, H.E. (1995) 'Cardiff and its port facilities' *Morgannwg* XXXIX, 50–71.

—. (1996) 'Cardiff's Norwegian heritage: a neglected theme' *Welsh History Review* 18 (2), 255–271.

Rowson, Stephen and Wright, Ian L. (2001) *The Glamorganshire and Aberdare Canals: Volume I Merthyr Tydfil and Aberdare to Pontypridd* (Lydney: Black Dwarf).

Slader, John (1988) *The Red Duster at War* (Kimber).

Smythe, W.H. (1840) *Nautical Observations on the Port and Maritime Vicinity of Cardiff* (Cardiff).

Stammers, M.K. (2000) 'Coal for the Cape, the *N.B. Lewis* at Cardiff 1887' *Maritime Wales* 21, 83–9.

— (2003) 'Turnbull's Register of Shipping, a snapshot of south Welsh shipowning in 1885' *Maritime Wales* 24, 115–132.

Starkey, David J. (Ed.) (1999) *Shipping Movements in the ports of the United Kingdom, 1871–1913: A Statistical Profile* (University of Exeter Press).

Stradling, Rob (1996) *Cardiff and the Spanish Civil War* (Butetown History and Arts Centre).

Stuckey, Peter J. (1977) *The Sailing Pilots of the Bristol Channel* (Bristol: Redcliffe).

Tennent, A.J. (1990) *British Merchant Ships sunk by U-boats in the 1914–1918 War* (published by the author).

— (2001) *British and Commonwealth Merchant ship Losses to Axis submarines 1939–1945* (Sutton).

Thomas, C. Mervyn (1974) 'The civil wars in Glamorgan' in Williams, Glanmor (Ed.) *Glamorgan County History* Volume IV, 257–278 (Glamorgan County History Trust).

Thomas, P.N. (1992) *British Ocean Tramps Volume 2: owners and their ships* (Waine Research Publications).

Thorne, Roy (1975) *Penarth–A History* (Risca: Starling Press).

Trounce, W.J. (1918) *Cardiff in the Fifties: the reminiscences of Alderman W.J. Trounce JP 1850–1860.* (Cardiff: Western Mail).

Tupper, Edward (1938) *Seamen's torch: the life story of Captain Edward Tupper* (Hutchinson).

Wall, Robert (1973) *Bristol Channel pleasure steamers* (Newton Abbot: David and Charles).

Watson, Richard (1997) *Rhondda Coal, Cardiff Gold: The Insoles of Llandaff, coal owners and shippers* (Merton Priory Press).

Willan, T.S. (1938) *The English Coasting Trade 1600–1750* (Manchester University Press).

Williams, D.H. (1984) *The Welsh Cistercians* (Caldy Island).

Williams, Desmond I. (1989) *Seventy years in shipping: some reminiscences of the history of Graig Shipping plc* (Barry: Graig Shipping Group/Stewart Williams).

Williams, J. (1985) *Digest of Welsh Historical Statistics* (Cardiff: Welsh Office).

Williams, John (1980) 'The coal industry 1750–1914' in John A.H. and Williams G. (Eds) *Glamorgan County History* Volume V, 155–210 (Glamorgan County History Trust).

Williams, Moelwyn I. (1959) 'Some aspects of the economic and social life of southern Glamorgan 1600–1800' *Morgannwg* III, 21–40.

Williams, Moelwyn I. (1963) 'Cardiff – its people and its trade 1660–1720' *Morgannwg* VII, 74–97.

Williams M.I. 'A contribution to the commercial history of Glamorgan' *National Library of Wales Journal* Volume IX: 188–215, 334–353; Volume XI: 330–360; Volume XII: 58–81. 265–287.

Woodward, Daniel (Ed.) (1973) 'Sir Thomas Button, the *Phoenix* and the defence of the Irish coast 1614–1622' *The Mariner's Mirror* 59 (2) 343–344.

INDEX